Where Do I Draw the Line?

Where Do I Draw the Line?

MICHAEL P. FARRIS

BETHANY HOUSE PUBLISHERS
MINNEAPOLIS, MINNESOTA 55438

Published by Bethany House Publishers
A Ministry of Bethany Fellowship, Inc.
6820 Auto Club Road, Minneapolis, Minnesota 55438

Printed in the United States of America

Library of Congress Cataloging-in-Publication Data

Farris, Michael P., 1951–
   Where do I draw the line?
     p. cm.

    1. Civil rights—Religious aspects—Christianity.
2. Christianity and law.
BT738.15.W44   1992
323.44'2'0973—dc20   92-9606
ISBN 1–55661–229–X   CIP

This book is dedicated to Dottie Roberts, Marcella Smith, and Eleanora Ballasiotes. When I was a young man, these three women, experienced from years of local and state political involvement, challenged me to stand up for what is right. They taught me many valuable lessons and then supported me with their prayers, gifts, and love.

MICHAEL P. FARRIS is a constitutional lawyer who has represented Christians in many of the best-known religious freedoms cases of the 1980s and early '90s. Some of these cases have been profiled on *60 Minutes* and other national-network news programs. He is the President and Founder of Home School Legal Defense Association, providing legal assistance to more than 15,000 home-schooling families. He and his family live in Virginia.

Contents

Pushed to the Limit

The phone rang late at night and on the line was a friend from the West Coast, who is the principal of a public high school. Larry[1] is under attack from liberal citizens' groups and the media because he had framed and hung on his office wall scripture verses such as: "A good name is more desired than riches." They claimed that his Christian views were invading the school in violation of "the separation of church and state"—and there was controversy over the fact that the school's choir was scheduled to sing *Messiah* by Handel.

The secularists convinced the school board to order the removal of any Christian materials in the school, even from private offices. *Messiah* was to be canceled.

Larry called me for both legal and spiritual counsel, not only because of my fifteen years of experience in constitutional litigation, but because in years past I'd been an elder in his church. We'd often talked about secularists' efforts to drive Christianity from the public schools. But this wasn't merely a topic of conversation. Larry was under attack. He needed to know how to stand up for his spiritual beliefs, and how to preserve his job. It was important to him to respond in a Christlike manner—yet he wanted to know his constitutional rights as well. I admired both his spirituality and his strength under fire. We talked late into the night.

Today, just like Larry, many others are under attack.

Christian parents are being told that they can *not* have a voice in the choice of textbooks their children read in the

---

[1]Not his real name. This problem is ongoing at the time of writing, so I have left out his name and city.

public schools. Churches are being told that they must adhere to the "norms of society" in the hiring of church staff—even if that means homosexuals can be forced upon a church congregation. Christian teachers are told they cannot have their Bible sitting on their desk in their classroom. If a porno theater moves into a neighborhood shopping area, and a Christian dares to complain, he'll be castigated as a "censor."

Christians are being pushed, harassed, or told to be silent. Many want to stand up for what they believe in, knowing that at some point they must draw the line. But for so many, like my friend Larry, the difficult question is—how?

Consider how just a few Christians have responded to the pressure of an increasingly hostile world.

Pushed Beyond the Limit

Evelyn Smith is a widow living in Sacramento, California. To supplement her modest income, she rented out a small dwelling. Based on her Christian principles and in an effort to be a good steward of her property, she decided she did not want to rent to smokers, unmarried couples, or homosexuals. When an unmarried couple tried to rent her place, she politely turned them down, refusing to be a party to their illicit cohabitation. Mrs. Smith thought she had the right to use her own property in a manner consistent with her convictions— but the state of California thought differently. She was served with legal papers and forced into litigation for "violating" one of California's liberal laws protecting the "right" of unmarried people to conduct their "alternative lifestyles." A Christian woman lost the right to decide what she would do with her own property.

An assistant professor of criminology at Memphis State University with a distinguished teaching record came under fire when he helped form a faculty/staff fellowship for Christians on the Tennessee campus. His response was to appeal, but after prolonged discussion the administration's decision made it clear that a Christian was simply not welcome on the MSU faculty: A good man was driven out of his job for an act as simple as encouraging Christian fellowship.

A mother in Spokane, Washington, was appalled to learn that her daughter had been leaving school to go downtown to obtain birth-control pills. School officials had assured her that the high school had a "closed campus" policy and that students could not leave school without their parents' permission. But word was circulated throughout the student body that a counselor would excuse you to go to the local family planning clinic: You could legally skip school and no one would ever tell your parents. This fourteen-year-old girl was a virgin, but she wanted to skip out of some classes one day. So she went to the counselor and was excused to go to the clinic, where she was given birth-control pills. A few days later she lost her virginity.

Several months later, she told her mother that since she had the pills anyway, she'd decided to put them to use. By the time this mother found out what was going on and what the school district had done to encourage her daughter into this lifestyle, substantial damage had already been done. The mother took a stand in public, exposing this situation so that other parents would be alerted to the danger before it was too late for them to protect their own children. And the harassment began.

In Hastings, Minnesota, the growing congregation of Cornerstone Bible Church wanted to use a vacant theater in a downtown commercial district. They were refused permission by city zoning officials, and federal courts upheld the city's decision to keep churches out of business districts. The church has kept on appealing in the courts, and a recent decision of a federal appeals court has given the church some reason to hope that they will eventually prevail. In the meantime, it has been a long and expensive process for this congregation to try to preserve the rights of their mission and ministry in Hastings.

In fifteen years of legal practice, I have witnessed dozens of cases in which Christians have been harassed, intimidated, threatened, and silenced. Once I represented a university student who was told he could not mention Christian principles in a business speech class when required to give a talk on ethics. Once I represented several Christians who were arrested for going door-to-door in a lawful and peaceful manner simply to invite people to attend their church. Once I represented a national campus ministry that was forbidden to hold a Bible study in a former fraternity house they rented near the University of Washington campus, because the building wasn't "zoned as a church." The city officials, however, saw no problem with the fraternity house next door hosting "keggers," even though it was not zoned as a tavern.

Daily, it seems, the attacks grow bolder and our liberties are increasingly in jeopardy. Christians feel themselves pushed beyond limits and, too often, do not know how to respond.

Encouragement in the Midst of Turmoil

There is good news to be found amid all of these troubling stories. In a number of the cases mentioned, the Christians eventually *won*. In fact, the vast majority of my years of legal practice has been dedicated to the principle: *Christians have rights,* given to us by God. Sometimes the courts agree, and we have emerged from the struggles with victories that are important not only to the individuals involved but to *all* of us.

Maybe you're one who says "amen" to the concept that "Christians have rights, too." Or you may, like so many Christians, have a real struggle with the idea of "rights." Since Scripture tells us we are "strangers in this world," we automatically assume that means we have no right to stand up for our beliefs here on earth. Some are taught that our troubles are a chastisement from God, and we should simply accept them. Most of us wonder if we shouldn't just "turn the other cheek," as Jesus instructed. These questions are important, and in Chapter 2 we'll look at the biblical principles that undergird a Christian's right to take a stand in the public arena. In Chapter 9, we will consider the importance of having the right spiritual attitudes when we are called upon to resist the world's pressure to violate our principles.

To begin, though, I must say I do not believe that Christians have any *more* rights than other citizens. Indeed, I've represented a number of non-Christians over the years, and have fought with equal vigor for their rights as parents, as taxpayers, and as citizens. Any morally minded citizen may eventually feel the harassment and pressure. But Christians have been the recipients of a disproportionate number of attacks from employers, government regulators, left-wing advocacy groups, public schools, and the media.

This book is written to help Christians know how to respond wisely in a practical sense, and in the right spirit. The truth is, most of us want to stand for what we really hold dear: our faith, our families, and our freedom. But often as Christians, we wrestle with spiritual principles that seem to suggest we must simply endure the rebuffs of the world. And so we'll deal with these dilemmas and provide clear answers from Scripture. Many times, for example, I have found Christians who are willing to protect their children, but they simply don't know the steps of action they should take in order to be most effective. The majority of this book deals with solid, practical advice, with principles and steps of action that will enable Christians to respond effectively and with integrity when faced with wrongful pressure coming from the institutions that are supposed to protect and serve us, and in our jobs, communities, and schools.

Why Are Christians Increasingly Under Attack?

The situation we see today has been developing over a number of years. At one time Christian values were welcome in every aspect of public life. In the early days of our nation, the Bible was the most-quoted book in the Congressional Record. Now Christians are the most-castigated minority on network television. The profound cultural shift this represents came gradually, as the result of many forces. A brief review may be helpful.

Francis Schaeffer offered the most succinct explanation for our nation's slide into its current cultural condition. Schaeffer wrote and lectured about the consequences of the competing humanistic and Christian world views. Built on the foundation of evolution, the humanist world view denies that there are any moral absolutes and contends that man holds within himself the solution to all problems. These ideas have real, practiced consequences. As Schaeffer wrote—and I have personally observed—these humanistic ideas have had a profound impact upon our legal system:

> Having no base for law, those who hold the humanist view make binding law whatever they personally think is good for society at the moment. This leads increasingly to arbitrary law and rulings which produce chaos in society and which then naturally and increasingly tend to lead to some form of authoritarianism. At that point, what the country had in the first place is lost and dead.[2]

We are not quite to the place where our nation's founding principles are "lost and dead," but we are well down that dangerous path. Most definitely, we are at a crossroads. The media and liberals like to describe the conflict in world views as "pluralism." But Schaeffer warned us that pluralism—that is, what the liberals mean by pluralism—is simply "the period of transition from one orthodoxy to another." And it's urgent that we remember this: The humanists are quite interested in establishing their own orthodoxy, which we will all be forced to live by.

In reality, Christians are being attacked simply because we represent a competing world view. Humanists are not tolerant of those who believe in moral absolutes. It's ironic that they preach tolerance of *sin,* but deny tolerance for those of us who stand upon the Christian principles that founded our nation. It is not "knee-jerk conservatism" to say that humanists want to control our nation, and *especially* our children. To accomplish their mission, they use tactics that attack and harass Christians and all others who believe in moral absolutes.

It is true that we Christians can too easily succumb to conspiracy theories; however, I do not see any evidence that

---

[2]Francis A. Schaeffer, *The Christian Manifesto* (Wheaton, Ill.: Crossway Books, 1981), p. 136.

attacks against Christians are orchestrated in any way. Rather, these attacks are the consequences of ideas that are being systematically taught in our schools and communicated through the mass media.

Ideas Become Reality

My friend Larry and I had often talked about the humanist world view and similar ideas. But when he faced his own attack, he did not need more discussion of ideas or world views. He needed to know how to respond.

Perhaps you find yourself pressed to respond on a different battlefront. Pushed into a situation not of your choosing, you feel ill-equipped.

- You may be a mother pressured to allow your children to be subjected to unprincipled sex education in the public school.
- You may be an employee facing a company demand to attend a New Age training seminar.
- Your church may be confronted with local efforts to establish a gay rights ordinance, which would not only affect the community, but could be used to invade the church itself.
- Your family may decide to home school your children and then face bureaucratic pressure to return your children to the public schools.

This book is written to give you a practical, step-by-step response to such situations. We will also look at the increasing efforts of bureaucrats to stop parents who desire to follow biblical principles of child rearing, and I will explain the best way to preserve your parental rights.

We will explore the areas where Christians today are feeling most pressured, and consider issues of employee rights, home schooling, church freedom, Christian schools, and more. Throughout this book, we will keep a dual focus on the best way to fight for your rights and freedoms, while maintaining a proper Christian spirit. This may sound like a contradiction—something like the "contradiction" of being a Christian attorney—but we can achieve this important balance. Our opponents love nothing better than to push us out of balance.

We can learn how to draw the line effectively and wisely. And it's my belief that standing against pressure and moral darkness *is* a part of the spiritual calling of every one of us.

What follows can be your tool for standing your ground and, even in the midst of struggle, knowing the support and guidance of the One who is our Counselor.

◇ **2** ◇

Citizens of Two Worlds

In the early 1980s, issues arose that caused many Christians to become active in the political process and in the public arena. At this time I was in Spokane, Washington, working as a trial attorney in a small firm with other Christian lawyers. Even prior to this, before my graduation from Gonzaga University Law School, I'd been involved in moral activism with others in the Christian community. After graduation I began working on local issues like pornography, which led to my involvement in a national lawsuit against the extra three and a half years Congress illegally allotted for the ratification of the Equal Rights Amendment. These activities allowed me the privilege of working more and more with local and national Christian leaders and organizations.

Ultimately, I left private practice to head a state-wide Christian political organization as well as serve as the General Counsel for Beverly LaHaye's organization, Concerned Women for America. We were fighting for the rights of parents to shield their children from sexually explicit films. Regularly, we were involved in battles for religious freedom—such as the defense of sixty-six worshipers expelled from Faith Baptist Church in Louisville, Nebraska—and constantly battled against abortion and pornography.

This kind of legal practice is necessarily confrontational and stirs controversy. I wasn't surprised, therefore, when I was attacked by the media, the ACLU, and similar groups. But there was one source of attack I never expected—other Christians. I was amazed at how often fellow Christians criticized what I was doing. I was told that believers should never be involved in such issues, that I should support the government and not criticize its policies—even when the policy in question was the pro-abortion position of the courts. I was told, "It's *unscriptural* to sue the government," even when one lawsuit involved a police raid on a church service!

At times the criticism was painful. For instance, the chairman of the board of elders in the church I was attending became very critical of my activities, especially when I stood against humanism in the public schools. He said, "Christians should not try to Christianize gentile structures." There were times I went home from church so discouraged I was ready to quit.

In Philippians, the apostle Paul reminds us that we have a "citizenship" in heaven. And yet he also exercised his own rights as a citizen of the Roman empire, as we'll see in a moment. I've come to believe that we cannot forsake our obligations or our rights as citizens of *this* world, simply claiming that our true home is in heaven. Yes, we must get our priorities straight, and yes, we must seek to grow in godly character—but that does not excuse us from acting on godly principles in public matters.

Even so, it's unfortunate but true: Too often, the toughest criticisms we have to endure come from other Christians. Vicki Frost, a courageous mother from Church Hill, Tennessee, stood up against a school district that wanted to force her children to read occultic and immoral textbooks. She had to endure horrific abuse from other professing Christians, and was driven from her church by their intense criticism.

Even though her case was extreme, I've found that most Christians who take a stand for right principles have been challenged by other professing Christians. Most of the challenges are not mean-spirited. Rather, they come from sincere, loving people who believe it's wrong to take a stand.

I understand why such opposition exists among Christians—it's based on their interpretation of certain scriptures. But I believe Scripture gives us broader views of our work in this world, and that there are scripturally based answers to the hard questions Christians raise. Many times we can win over our critics by simply answering their legitimate questions.

There is a second reason why we need to be able to answer tough questions. If we are challenged by other believers, we can begin to doubt ourselves and wonder whether we really are making a mistake in the eyes of God. That's why it is important to understand the scriptural principles involved in taking a stand *before* you enter a public confrontation. When you're trying to resist the pressures of the world, you need to be able to answer criticisms quickly and move on. If you allow criticism to throw you into a tailspin of self-doubt, you'll become bogged down in your effort to protect your children, your faith, or your freedom. This is not to say that you should ignore *all* criticism, nor have the attitude that "I'm always right." But for now I want to focus on the general criticism that "Christians should not be involved in these kinds of battles." People will say this to you with all sincerity; I believe that they are sincerely wrong.

Let's consider the five most common questions.

Five Questions

1. *When do we "stand up for beliefs," and when do we "turn the other cheek"?*

There are two concepts found in Scripture that seem contradictory: On one hand we're told to stand up for righteousness, while on the other hand we're told to turn the other cheek to those who want to do evil toward us. How do we sort out these seeming inconsistencies?

Let's begin with a look at the scripture passages:

> But I [Jesus] tell you, Do not resist an evil person. If someone strikes you on the right cheek, turn to him the other also. And if someone wants to sue you and take your tunic, let him have your cloak as well. If someone forces you to go one mile, go with him two miles. Give to the one who asks you, and do not turn away from the one who wants to borrow from you. You have heard that it was said, "Love your neighbor and hate your enemy." But I tell you: Love your enemies and pray for those who persecute you. (Matthew 5:39–44)
>
> Who will rise up for me against the wicked? Who will

take a stand for me against evildoers? (Psalm 94:16)

Have nothing to do with the fruitless deeds of darkness, but rather expose them. (Ephesians 5:11)

In the passage from the Sermon on the Mount, Jesus was teaching the proper response to our personal enemies. Let's say your child is being forced to read an occultic textbook in the public school, and when you go and talk with the principal he says, "You're being ridiculous to be so concerned about your child. Lighten up, it's just a story." That is a personal insult, and we should endure such insults without striking back. That is a time for a "soft answer" that can turn away his wrath. (See Proverbs 15:1.)

On the other hand, it doesn't mean that you should succumb to his desire to have your child read the offending book. You should still "take a stand" for God against "evildoers." You should still insist that your child not be subjected to "the fruitless deeds of darkness."

Two episodes from the life of David illustrate when we should respond with firm conviction and when we should turn the other cheek.

When David was king, he was confronted by a man named Shimei. Shimei insisted on cursing David and his men and pelting them with small stones. David's men wanted to kill Shimei as a fitting response to one who cursed the king. But David would not allow them to harm Shimei despite the taunts. David recognized that the curses could have come from God's rebuke and he left it to God to bless him if he had been cursed unjustly. (See 2 Samuel 16:5–14.) This is a classic case of an unjustified personal attack. David turned the other cheek.

Once, I was in a debate with a historian from the University of Mississippi, making a point about the Christian heritage of this country. I used an illustration from Samuel Adams, mentioning that Adams had been the governor of Massachusetts. The historian broke in and said, "Samuel Adams was never the governor of Massachusetts"—which caused the crowd to laugh at me. It happened that I was right about Adams—but it was best to ignore the personal slam and debate the principles. I let the insult go by.

Earlier in David's life, though, he also gave us a clear example of when to give a strong response to an adversary. David responded with courage and conviction when he killed Goliath, whose taunts came against the person and character of God. David framed the question correctly when he asked what right an uncircumcised Philistine had that he should defy the armies of *the living God* (1 Samuel 17:26).

If we are confronted with issues that defy God's principles, loyalty to our faith and Christian mission, or our duty to protect our children—we need to stand resolutely on the side of biblical principles.

2. *What if we are confronted by a government official—doesn't Scripture say we're supposed to obey the government?*

It is true that, as a general rule, Christians are to obey the governing authorities. Paul clearly proclaims: "Everyone must submit himself to the governing authorities, for there is no authority except that which God has established" (Romans 13:1). But even in Scripture, we see that this general rule has exceptions.

Daniel disobeyed the governors of Babylon when he refused to eat the king's meat and drink the king's wine. (See Daniel 1.) Shadrach, Meshach and Abednego defied the king of Babylon to his face when they were required to bow down before the idol the king had erected. And Daniel continued to pray to God in disobedience to the order of the king, and he ended up in the lions' den as a result. The apostle Paul was commanded by the ruling Jewish council to stop teaching in the name of Jesus. Paul's response to this command was: "We must obey God rather than men" (Acts 5:29). If we face a situation where we are required to do something we don't like for personal reasons, our duty is still to obey. But if we are confronted with something that will require us to violate one of God's commands or principles, then our duty is quite the opposite: We are not to succumb to any violation of His standards.

As citizens in a democratic society, there is another matter we must consider in order to fully understand how important it is to stand up for what is right—even if it involves confrontation with a government official: Our duty is to obey *the law* of man unless it violates the law of God. But under a constitutional system, there is often a legitimate question of whether the action of a government official accurately reflects the law of man.

Here are two important rules of law you must know:

First, you are not required to obey an order from a government official that is unauthorized by law. In my work with home schoolers, for instance, this situation arises constantly. School officials often make a demand that is simply unauthorized by law. By way of example, Pennsylvania law requires students to be tested in grades 3, 5, and 8. Despite this clear law, the superintendent of the Pittsburgh School District demanded that home-schooled students be tested more than twelve times *each year* ! We tried to appeal to him, but he stood firm. We took him to court and the judge ruled that the superintendent was breaking the law because he had no authority to demand all those extra tests.

Second, you are not required to obey an official's order that is unconstitutional. When I was in law school I led an effort to keep the city of Spokane from establishing a tavern in the middle of a city park and a liquor lounge in the city opera house that was on the edge of the same park. I was standing in front of the city opera house one night gathering signatures on a petition to try to stop the tavern. The manager of the opera house obviously opposed my efforts and he called the police, who told me to stop gathering signatures. After talking politely with the police for a couple of minutes, I told them that they were interrupting my effort to gather signatures and their order was unconstitutional. I told them that if they insisted on stopping me, I would be forced to sue them and the city for their unconstitutional action. They got into their police car and called someone on the radio—who apparently told them that I was right—and they left. The next day, I even received an apology from a higher police official.

Paul exemplified this same strategy when officials wanted to flog him. He stood on his rights as a Roman citizen and claimed, "Is it legal for you to flog a Roman citizen who hasn't even been found guilty?" (Acts 22:25).

We must remember that under our legal system, a government official who demands something that is unauthorized or unconstitutional is the one who is breaking the law. We are entitled to stand on our rights as citizens. A word of caution: Get good legal advice any time you suspect the action of an official may be either unauthorized or unconstitutional. If you guess wrong on this, there could be important consequences.

3. *Should we advocate laws that are based on principles in the Old Testament when we're now in the age of grace?*

Your city may find itself embroiled in a battle over a proposed law that wants to give special rights to homosexuals, or condone abortion, or permit pornography. If you stand up in a church meeting and urge that your congregation help put a stop to such immorality, you may be confronted with this question: Should we try to impose God's principles, which were intended for ancient Israel, upon modern America? How do you answer such a question?

First, you can point out that God clearly declares His intention for all nations to obey His moral principles, not just Israel. Through the prophet Jeremiah, God proclaimed:

> If at any time I announce that a nation or kingdom is to be uprooted, torn down and destroyed, and if that nation I warned repents of its evil, then I will relent and not inflict on it the disaster I had planned. And if at another time I announce that a nation or kingdom is to be built up and planted, and if it does evil in my sight and does not obey me, then I will reconsider the good I had intended to do for it. (Jeremiah 18:7–10)

On the other hand, there are those who advocate the idea that America should enact the *Old Testament* law right down to the rules for conducting trials. I am not one of those people, but I do believe the moral principles of God apply to every age. The principles of the Ten Commandments, for example, will forever be valid and should be honored in modern America.

It's also important to remember that the founders of this country believed that the principles in God's Word should be used in our nation. The laws of Massachusetts once proclaimed: "The ordinances of Jesus Christ shall be enforced by the magistrate in every community." The first written constitution in the history of mankind, the Fundamental Orders of Connecticut, declared:

> . . . [And] well knowing where a people are gathered together the word of God requires that to maintain the peace and union of such a people there should be an orderly and decent government established according to God, to order and dispose of the affairs of the people at all seasons as occasion shall require; [we] do therefore associate and conjoin ourselves to be as one Public State or commonwealth; and do, for ourselves and our successors and such as shall be adjoined to us at any time hereafter, enter into combination and confederation together, to maintain and preserve the liberty and purity of the gospel of our Lord Jesus which we now profess, as also the discipline of the Churches, which according to the truth of the said gospel is now practiced amongst us; as also in our civil affairs to be guided and governed according to such laws, rules, orders and decrees as shall be made, ordered and decreed. . . .

In order to hold office in Delaware, the Constitution of 1776 in that state required the following oath:

> I, _____ , do profess faith in God the Father, and in Jesus Christ His only Son, and in the Holy Ghost, one God, blessed for evermore; and I do acknowledge the Holy Scriptures in the Old and New Testament to be given by divine inspiration.

The founding fathers of this nation boldly employed the Word of God in the public arena. As a matter of strategy, which we will discuss in a later chapter, it is often better to simply talk about right and wrong without quoting Scripture or "beating people over the heads with our Bibles." But this is quite different than saying that the principles of God's Word no longer apply to our nation. Right and wrong hasn't changed in God's eyes. It shouldn't change in ours either.

4. *Shouldn't we honor the separation of church and state?*

This particular question is one that is repeatedly asked by liberals who want to stop Christian involvement. But there are many of your fellow believers who are confused by it as well. You need to be able to answer this question no matter who asks it.

First, let's consider the real origin of the phrase "separation of church and state." Thomas Jefferson coined this phrase, which is so often misused, in a letter to a Baptist church in Connecticut. Read what Chief Justice William Rehnquist recently wrote about the origin of this phrase:

> It is impossible to build sound constitutional doctrine upon a mistaken understanding of constitutional history, but unfortunately the Established Clause has been expressly freighted with Jefferson's misleading metaphor for nearly forty years. Thomas Jefferson was of course in France at the time the constitutional Amendments known as the Bill of Rights were passed by Congress and ratified by the States. His letter to the Danbury Baptist Association was a short note of courtesy, written fourteen years after the Amendments were passed by Congress. He would seem to any detached observer as a less than ideal source of contemporary history as to the meaning of the Religion Clauses of the First Amendment.[1]

The error over Jefferson's letter is even more apparent when this "short note of courtesy" is examined in light of its historical context. The Danbury Baptist Association had written to Jefferson to ask him to declare a national day of thanksgiving, as George Washington and John Adams had both done during their tenure as president. Jefferson declined to do so, saying he believed that such a declaration would violate the "separation of church and state." Specifically, Jefferson was arguing that a government had no power to declare a holiday that pointed people to God.

Although the liberals like to cite Thomas Jefferson, the

---

[1] *Wallace* v. *Jaffree,* 472 U.S. 92 (1985).

actual author of the First Amendment was James Madison. While Jefferson was serving in France at the time the Bill of Rights was written, Madison was serving in Congress. He was the driving force behind the Bill of Rights, and the First Amendment in particular. When Madison was president, he followed Washington and Adams in declaring a national day of thanksgiving to God. A friend wrote him to ask him why he'd declared this day of religious worship, since he'd been such a staunch defender of religious liberty. Madison wrote back, saying that it was not unconstitutional for the government to have a day set aside to honor God so long as no person was ever coerced to participate.

Madison's balanced view represents the accurate meaning of the First Amendment: *The government is free to acknowledge God in a nonsectarian manner, but no person can ever be forced to participate in a religious activity.*

Although the courts have used Jefferson's phrase, they have stopped short of fully embracing Jefferson's radical interpretation of the First Amendment. Even in modern times, the ACLU was unsuccessful in their attempt to get a federal court to overrule President Reagan's declaration of the Year of the Bible as unconstitutional. I wrote a brief in that case, supporting President Reagan's declaration. As a result I appeared on a talk show in Los Angeles and debated with representatives from the ACLU. During that show I was able to coax the ACLU to admit that they believed it was unconstitutional to have a national day of thanksgiving to God. If Jefferson's opinion about a day of thanksgiving was wrong to begin with, then the metaphor he used to support that position is equally wrong.

The First Amendment does say that Congress "should make no law respecting an establishment of religion." This means that we should not have a state church, nor anything else that smacks of an official religion. But nonsectarian references to God, such as in the pledge of allegiance, on our money, and prayers in Congress do not violate this provision.

Liberals have used the "separation of church and state" argument to try to prevent Christians from being involved in government. They argue that religious people have no right to be in politics because they will inherently bring their religion with them. The United States Supreme Court disagrees. In *McDaniel* v. *Paty,* 435 U.S. 618 (1978), the Court held that a Baptist minister had the constitutional right to run for public office despite a provision in the Tennessee state constitution that barred ministers from holding public office. Normally it is better for Christian laymen to run for office than for full-time pastors to leave their congregation and enter politics. But if pastors have the constitutional right to hold elected office, any claim that Christians cannot fully participate in public affairs because of the "separation of church and state" is patently ridiculous.

There is nothing unconstitutional about God nor those who worship God. We shouldn't let a mere slogan deprive us of our birthright as American citizens. This is One Nation Under God and we have an equal right and responsibility to participate in this nation.

5. *Why should we work for good laws? Shouldn't we just be presenting the gospel—changing hearts instead of changing the law?*

The job of first importance for every church and every Christian is to seek out those who need salvation in Jesus Christ. But that is not our *only* job. We never hear people arguing that we shouldn't take the time to be good parents and train our children. "Just get the kids saved; there's no need to teach them the principles of right and wrong." No one would be so foolish to make such an argument.

Jesus clearly tells us that we are to be the salt of the earth and the light of the world (Matthew 5:13–16). To be the salt of the earth means that we are to act as agents for purifying society, just as salt is an agent to keep meat pure. If the salt doesn't do its job, society goes rotten. It's not pleasant to face, but one reason there is much moral depravity in our nation is that we, as the salt of the earth, have often neglected our job. As light of the world, we are to proclaim God's truth against the encroaching darkness.

As Christians, then, we have multiple duties. Evangelism is certainly a task of the first order. But we are also called to be salt and light in society. Jesus admonished us:

> You are the light of the world. A city on a hill cannot be hidden. Neither do people light a lamp and put it under a bowl. Instead they put it on its stand, and it gives light to everyone in the house. In the same way, let your light shine before men, that they may see your good deeds and praise your Father in heaven. (Matthew 5:14–16)

We can see from this passage that we are called to be light, and to *use* our light.

Weapons That Work

Most people are willing to stand up for their convictions. But too often, we simply do not know the best way to respond. Moreover, we don't want to come off as small-minded, overzealous or judgmental.

At times I've cringed with embarrassment when hearing Christians stand before a public body like a school board or city council, saying, "God will judge you if you vote the wrong way." Once I saw a man deliver a speech before a state legislative committee, clearly implying that God would take the life or health of any member of that committee who refused to vote in favor of the bill he wanted. His speech was an embarrassment to the rest of us who favored the bill, and it contributed to the bill's ultimate defeat.

As Christians, we need to know how to be wise and effective in our speaking. And yet it's a far greater problem when good people fail to speak up simply because they don't know what to say.

There is a way we can be sure that we're fighting for our principles with weapons of integrity and honesty. In fact, to maintain the best Christian witness, it's urgent that our strategies be strong and good.

After more than a decade of involvement in battles in the context of legal and political issues and in the media, I've learned the hard way how best to respond. Other lessons have come from observing and working with leaders of some national Christian organizations.

Learning From Our Mistakes

I have had the privilege of knowing personally and working with almost all of the prominent Christians who are awakening believers to the need to be involved in moral and family concerns. All of these leaders have demonstrated a sincere and pure heart in their desire to take a stand for what is right. They have realized their involvement could very well cause them to suffer significant harm in other areas of ministry because of their stand on moral issues. But they all did it anyway, because they knew it was right.

Yet it's true to say there were mistakes, and we can learn from these. At times, statements were issued to the press that were not well thought out, and which caused a huge backlash. For example, once a leading pastor proclaimed that he was going to sponsor a "new and improved Equal Rights Amendment" once the original ERA was defeated. He was attacked by the feminists, and was criticized by those of us active on the anti-ERA side as well. We had been successful convincing state legislatures that the Constitution already gave legitimate equal protection to men and women. By talking about a "new ERA" he unintentionally managed to alienate everyone. Sometimes projects have been launched that were focused on issues of secondary importance, often doomed to fail because of faulty political analysis.

But when all is said and done, somebody had to blaze the trail, and all of us owe a great debt to the leaders who awakened the sleeping giant of Bible-believing Christians. We need not be put off by human error, and we can learn from their courage as well as their mistakes and victories.

Here are some simple "weapons" that will work.

"Weapons"

1. *Know what you are talking about.*

In 1975 I was given a petition which claimed that Madalyn Murray O'Hair had filed a request with the FCC for the purpose of eliminating all Christian programs on radio and television. I was incensed and wanted to help. I later learned that it was all phony. O'Hair had never filed such a petition—it was a blatant hoax.

But the poor workers in the FCC mail room have received hundreds of thousands of pieces of mail, containing millions of signatures in response to this nonexistent issue. Christians have come off looking very foolish in this episode. And we have wasted an enormous amount of time and money in the process. I still see this petition in circulation today.

If you hear of an issue that you would like to respond to, *ask questions first.* Don't be satisfied by calling Aunt Mildred who heard about it from her Christian hairdresser, or your friend down the street. If you are concerned about a proposed government policy, contact the government agency yourself and make sure there is such a policy. If they say it's true, then get a copy of any written materials and read them carefully. If they deny that there is such a proposal, you may have to dig deeper to be certain you are being told the truth.

Another excellent way to verify information is to contact a reputable organization that deals in such matters. For example, if you are concerned about an abortion issue, contact Christian Action Council. If there is a family policy issue, the Family Research Council, a division of Focus on the Family, is an excellent organization. Concerned Women for America can supply information on a broad range of issues, especially efforts involving family issues. For home-schooling matters, you may want to turn to the Home School Legal Defense Association for help. (At the end of this book there is an appendix, listing organizations that can give you further help.) Don't expect any organization to know every detail of every issue. But if they do not have an answer for you, they can usually give sound guidance on how to find the answer.

If the area of concern is of a more personal nature—for example, your child comes home from school and tells you something that turns your hair gray, *check it out first.* You need to believe your child enough to verify the report, but there are often misunderstandings and simple mistakes in communication. Give people a chance to explain before you launch countermeasures.

A man I know learned that his child's high-school science

teacher was not only teaching evolution but stifling all discussion that would question the truth of this theory. Upon checking, however, the parent found that the teacher was being forced to teach evolution, and not only did the teacher allow contrary discussion, he actually encouraged it. The child had misunderstood. This Christian parent saved himself great embarrassment by not going in with "guns blazing."

There will also be times when you find out important information that helps you fight back if you simply ask. I was once asked to verify a quotation by Dr. Chester Pierce, an educational psychologist from Harvard. The alleged quote, from a speech given to the Aspen Institute, was this:

> Every child in America entering school at the age of five is insane, because he comes to school with certain allegiances toward our founding fathers, toward our elected officials, toward his peers, toward a belief in a supernatural being, toward the sovereignty of this nation as a separate entity. It's up to you teachers to make all of these sick children well by creating the international children of the future.

I was able to verify that Pierce had delivered a speech to the Aspen Institute. I even found a published summary of the speech. But I could not find the precise quote. So I called Pierce himself, left a message, and he called me back—collect. He stated that he probably didn't use the term "insane" but said "mentally ill" instead. Other than that, he was happy to affirm that he made the statement.

Another time, a government secretary sent me documents that were helpful in our lawsuit fighting the ERA extension, documents showing the government had engaged in some questionable acts. I simply called and asked, and she mailed them to me.

Remember, your reputation is on the line when you confront someone about a problem. Verified information is a weapon that works.

2. *Don't be overwhelmed by "the system"—learn how it works.*

If you have a complaint about a city issue, for example, your first step is to learn some information about your city government. Is this a matter for the mayor's office, or for a city council member? Are the council members elected at large or by districts? Is this a matter that has been delegated to a department or agency?

These are the kinds of questions you should learn to ask. And it is surprisingly easy to learn the answers. Here's how this can work to your benefit.

Suppose you are concerned about a report you heard on the radio concerning your city's thinking of allowing alcohol to be consumed in city parks.

Step 1: The first thing to ask is, What agency would most likely be making the decision? And what agency would have information about the issue? Most likely, the city council would be making the decision. But it's also likely that the parks department would be the best source of information. Start with a phone call to the parks department: "I heard a report on WXXX radio that the city is considering allowing alcohol in the city parks. Whom could I speak with to obtain more information about this?"

Initially, ask for more information. Don't waste your time telling a receptionist your position on the issue unless she asks for your opinion. Usually you'll be told something like, "Bob Johnson is handling that matter." Your goal then is to speak to him.

Step 2: Before you launch into your opinion, ask "Bob Johnson" for details about the process. When will the decision be made? Who will make the decision? What events have led up to this? Who has recommended that this new policy be adopted? If "Bob Johnson" is not the decision maker, but has played a role in recommending the new policy (which is often the case), briefly share your opinion with him.

Your conversation with him has probably revealed most of the procedural details you will need to know. If he tells you the city council is going to make a decision, you'll need to determine the best way to communicate your views to the appropriate people on the city council. The way to do this is to call the city council office and ask (if you don't know) whether or not the city is divided into city council districts. If so, then you need the name and number or address of the person representing the district you live in.

With two phone calls like this you will almost always learn enough about the process to be a genuine expert on the system of decision making for this issue.

Step 3: Express your opinion to the decision maker in writing, on the phone, or in a public hearing, whichever you are most comfortable with and seems most effective. Letters almost always work very well.

If you take ten to fifteen minutes to learn the system, you can avoid the error of expressing your opinion to a person who has no ability to make a decision. If you ask a few questions so that you know *who* will make the decision, *when* the decision will be made, and *how* to contact the decision maker, you will have the opportunity to make your opinion heard in a manner that makes a difference. Knowing the system is a weapon that works.

3. *Pick the right target—and then appeal.*

If your child comes home from school and tells you that his teacher says he cannot pray silently over his lunch, whom would you talk with? In this case, it would be best to talk with the teacher first.

If the teacher verifies the story, then what do you do? Find out why she made the decision. If she made the decision on her own and won't change based solely on your appeal, go to her supervisor, the school principal. But if she tells you that she is merely enforcing a policy issued by the school superintendent, then don't waste your time talking with the principal—go straight to the superintendent.

Let's assume that the superintendent will not budge; what do you do? You go to his "boss," which is the school board. You are going to need to find a way to get directly to the school board rather than going through the superintendent. Go in person to a meeting, though you may have difficulty getting on the agenda unless you live in a very small community. If you live in a small or middle-sized community, you can contact school-board members at their homes or offices. If you live in a large city, school-board members usually have offices sufficiently independent of the superintendent that you can call them directly.

Many of the problems I have worked on over the years have been solved by simply appealing to a person's supervisor. And don't be afraid to keep appealing to the very highest levels. Don't stop your chain of appeals with the local school board. A phone call to the state department of education's legal department is a very good place to appeal if you think the policy is blatantly in error.

In the last chapter, I mentioned my effort to stop the city of Spokane from opening two taverns, one in a city park and another in the city opera house. I wasn't getting any satisfaction from the city council. In fact, some members of the city council ridiculed me when I spoke to the council. I was in law school at the time and some of my classmates also ridiculed me, but their jibes were much more good-natured. I didn't give up, though. With a little more research I found out that the state liquor control board would not license a facility in a park. With one letter to the state board, I won the battle against the proposed tavern in the park. Today, there is an ice cream parlor there instead, and it's enjoyed by a lot of families who probably know nothing whatever about my letter and appeal.

By continuing to appeal and by aiming as high as possible, I was able to prevail in that particular battle. Appealing your concern to the highest level is another weapon that works.

4. *Don't be a "lone ranger."*

When I was battling the two taverns, I was essentially fighting the battle alone. I announced a meeting to form a coalition to help with the effort. Although it was announced in the press and circulated to some churches, only one lady showed up at the meeting. Nonetheless, I formed Citizens Opposed to Opera house Liquor (COOL). When I spoke in public I did so on behalf of COOL. And the press duly reported the activities of COOL as an organization of citizens— and indeed the two of us were very organized.

As I have worked over the years, I have discovered that a

great number of organizations have very small memberships: Liberals are particularly good at forming organizations that have large names and small numbers.

It is obviously a good thing to have a number of people working together on an issue. If you are appealing to your local grocery store to remove *Playboy* magazine, three mothers going together to meet the manager will have a much more significant impact than if one goes alone. Two fathers going together to see a school principal will produce ten times the pressure that one father could muster on his own.

In a number of my court cases, I have represented groups of parents upset with some school-district policy. While interviewing the parents for the case I have often found that when they went in one-by-one to make their complaint, school officials told each and every one of them that they were "the only person" who had ever complained. If they had gone in together, the school officials could never have intimidated these parents by making them think they were lone voices. Your opponents will try to make you feel as if you are all alone as a means of intimidating you into silence. Don't buy it.

Some officials are so calloused that they remind me of the famous story from about the turn of the century of a man who wrote to the president of a railroad company. The man complained that he'd been bitten by bedbugs in his sleeping compartment. The president wrote back saying that this was the first incident ever reported of bedbugs in the history of the railroad. He wrote that he was appreciative of his concern and as a result of his complaint he was ordering fumigation for every sleeping car in the entire railroad. Unfortunately, in the envelope with the typed letter to the passenger was also the handwritten note to the president's secretary that declared: "Send this (expletive!) the bedbug letter."

If you believe that your issue is likely to end up in the media, I recommend that you form an organization and give yourself a name. It doesn't take a great number of people to have a strong impact. And having a small group will almost always be better than standing alone.

This does not mean you shouldn't stand alone if it comes

to that. For instance, I was attending the Washington State Bar Association Convention in 1977 when a group of liberals and feminists urged the association to join in the boycott of states that had not ratified the ERA. I had no advance notice that the issue was going to be on the agenda, and when it was debated, a number of lawyers spoke in favor of the boycott. Of the hundreds of lawyers present, I was the only one who spoke in opposition. But when the vote was taken, the group voted strongly against the ERA boycott. Apparently, I wasn't alone, though many later admitted they simply didn't have the courage to speak out.

Standing alone is sometimes necessary, and many times works. Nonetheless, I strongly recommend that you work with others whenever possible. Teamwork is a weapon that works.

5. *Choose battles that count.*

Sometimes Christians choose to fight insignificant matters. A friend was once involved in a public dispute with (believe it or not) a bakery selling "pornographic cookies." I agreed with him in the sense that the bakery shouldn't do that. But if a simple conversation with the owner didn't work, it would probably only end up as a waste of time and a source of embarrassment.

A well-known Christian legal organization once filed a "friend of the court" brief supporting a man from Virginia who wanted to have the word "atheist" on his license plate. They did so because it was a matter of religious freedom. Even though they were probably right as a matter of abstract constitutional law, I believe that it was a waste of time and money to write, print, and file the brief. There are so many important battles out there, why get involved with the atheists and license plates?

Frankly, I don't like to be confronted with *National Enquirer* or *Star* magazines at grocery store checkout lines with headlines about "sex nymphs," "Elvis reincarnated," or "crystal power." But other than expressing my opinion to the store manager, there is little I can do that is likely to be effective. I want to spend my time taking on issues that count.

Actually, this is a very good way to determine whether a particular organization is worth supporting. Ask yourself: What are they spending their time and money to accomplish? If they are going to "fight homosexuality by sending petitions to the President," save your money. The President seldom reads petitions, and one on the general issue of homosexuality will have no effect whatsoever on public policy. If there is a bill pending in Congress concerning gay rights, then by all means write to the President and to Congress. But generalized concerns about abstract problems do not make a lot of difference.

A series of questions will help you pick out battles that count.

- Will my action help advance a long-range objective of importance to me?
- Is there any chance that I can succeed?
- Is there some other project I could choose that would more effectively advance the same goal?

Don't limit yourself to working on an issue only when you know you can win. It is just as important to stand up for what's right, even if you don't believe you can win. But don't waste your time with an issue that would not be of significance even if you did win. You should make sure that the time, effort, and money you spend on a project bears some reasonable relation to the importance of the potential victory.

There is one issue that has consumed an enormous amount of Christians' time and resources over the years, and I believe it needs closer examination. That issue is prayer in the public schools. The Supreme Court decision that banned prayer in schools was issued in 1962. That is fully three decades ago. While Christians have focused enormous resources working to reverse that decision, the secularists have changed the entire face of the public school system through values clarification, evolution, permissive sex education, and other programs that focus on the five-hours-and-fifty-nine minutes that follow the opening one minute of the school day.

We have to ask ourselves if a minute of prayer—prayer

that is likely to be so watered down as to be of questionable value—is worth the effort, especially in light of the energy that could be spent on issues that have a greater chance of success. It is very hard to reverse a decision of the Supreme Court. In fact, there are only two ways to reverse a Supreme Court decision: through Congress, either by legislation or a constitutional amendment; or by getting new justices on the Supreme Court. All other efforts are a waste of time. However, a decision to implement sex education or values clarification is usually made by a school board. It is much easier to have a significant impact on such decisions.

Pick a battle that will mean something to you and your family both *now* and in the *future*. Use as your weapon the effectiveness of focusing on a goal that is worth the time and effort.

6. *Know whom to listen to.*

One of the first lessons I learned working in matters of public concern was this: Your friends are not always your friends, and your enemies are not always your enemies.

For instance, Terry Dolan was very influential in Washington, D.C., in the early 1980s as the president of National Conservative Political Action Caucus. He was very conservative on a number of issues, but he was soft on the issue of gay rights. A few years later the reason became apparent— Terry Dolan was dying of AIDS. Secretly, he'd been a practicing homosexual.

George Will, the noted conservative columnist, is an outspoken opponent of religious freedom. He has written that the reason our country was founded was to establish the "primacy of capitalism" over religion. He has urged the Supreme Court to reverse the decision of *Wisconsin* v. *Yoder,* which guarantees parents the right to give their children a religious education. He thinks parents should be forced to educate their children in public schools even if that violates their religious beliefs.

Robert Bork was no friend of Christian principles, though he was supported by many Christians in his potential nomination to the Supreme Court. When he was Solicitor General of the United States, he stopped the United States Attorney from Memphis from continuing his legal effort to prosecute the pornographic movie *Deep Throat.* In his writings, he also takes a very strong position *against* the view most Christians would hold on religious freedom.

Christians need to be careful in evaluating our "friends" based on the labels they carry. The term "conservative" means a lot of different things to different people. We should work together on specific projects with those who agree with us, but we should avoid blind loyalty to those who agree with us on a few issues.

The same kind of caution is appropriate in terms of our "enemies" as well. The American Civil Liberties Union is usually considered "Public Enemy No. 1" by Christians, and they certainly deserve that reputation, by and large. They favor abortion, pornography, special legal benefits for homosexuals, and they oppose any reference to God in public life. But they also are strong advocates of the free exercise of religion. They have filed a number of briefs *in favor* of Christians who home school their children. In 1980, the ACLU also filed briefs supporting the right of Moral Majority of Washington to publish their views about state political candidates.

In the early 1980s, I represented a group of pastors who were the victims of a police raid on a church prayer service in Louisville, Nebraska. We filed a civil rights case in federal court, alleging that the raid violated the constitutional rights of those believers. The case ended up in the U.S. Court of Appeals for the Eighth Circuit. And to my great pleasure we won. The judge who wrote the majority opinion was a liberal appointed by Jimmy Carter. The judge who dissented was a conservative appointed by President Reagan. The labels "conservative" and "liberal" aren't much more helpful than the terms "Republican" and "Democrat." There is a wide variety of beliefs held by people who wear each of these labels.

Whatever issue you are caught up in, learn to work with people on an issue-by-issue basis and avoid becoming permanently entrenched in any group that is not solidly founded on biblical principles—even if it calls itself Christian.

Christians need to guide their activities by principle, not personality. If the ACLU is arguing on behalf of a bill in your state legislature and a noted conservative organization is against it, you are wise to be suspicious about the bill. But that is simply not enough information to make a final judgment. Find out more about the bill itself and ask Christians who specialize in the issue what they think. And then make your own decision based upon the principles you believe in from God's Word.

7. *Don't accept trinkets.*

Christians worked very hard to get Ronald Reagan elected. We wanted an end to abortion. We wanted help in protecting the women and children of our nation from the exploitation of pornography. We wanted a return to principles of honoring God in our national life. We also helped George Bush get elected for many of the same reasons.

What's been the reward for Christians for our political help and support? Some of our leaders have been invited to the White House. One year was declared "the Year of the Bible." Some of our Christian leaders have had their picture taken with the President. We've had some studies, we've had some committees. We have gotten a bunch of political trinkets. But we have had very little real progress in terms of advancing our public policy goals or getting our kind of people appointed to positions of real influence.

The temptation to accept trinkets comes at all levels. If a pastor gets active in opposing a city government's effort to allow pornographic theaters, he will probably receive an invitation to play a leading role at the mayor's prayer breakfast. If a mother launches an especially effective campaign against a humanistic textbook, the superintendent will often appoint that mother to an advisory committee for the school district.

Don't get me wrong. One of the most important things we can do to affect public policy is to have good personal relationships with leaders. But liberals have good personal relationships with leaders and yet they have the wisdom to not accept political trinkets. They go to the dinners. They attend

the receptions. However, they also demand key appoint-
ments and they get public policy changes.

We shouldn't sell all of our hard work for a pot of red
lentils.

8. *Know the difference between partial victories and compromise.*

Politicians love the word "compromise."

On the other hand, many Christians have been trained to
hate compromise. They view a compromise as "selling out"
to the enemy. And in many cases what is called "compromise" really would require us to violate our principles, so
this is indeed a delicate matter.

But I believe that we Christians are politically naive and
spiritually misguided to think that anything less than immediate, total victory is unacceptable. If we can't ban all abortions, for example, we won't support a bill that bans 99 percent of abortions. I think there is clear biblical support for
working toward gradual or partial victories. And I think there
is a difference between accepting a partial victory and an
improper compromise.

When the children of Israel were entering the Promised
Land, they were commanded to drive out the enemy from
the land. But were they supposed to do this all at once? Here's
what God said to them:

> But I will not drive them out in a single year, because
> the land would become desolate and the wild animals
> too numerous for you. Little by little I will drive them
> out before you, until you have increased enough to take
> possession of the land. (Exodus 23:29–30)

We can be fully in God's will and still be obtaining our
victories one step at a time.

How do we tell the difference between a partial victory
and a compromise? The root of the word *compromise* holds
the key. That word, of course, is "promise." If your support
of a less-than-ideal solution to a problem requires you to
promise to abide by this solution now and in the future, that
is a compromise.

For example, I don't like pornography—not any kind of pornography. But if I were in a legislature and had a chance to vote for a very important bill banning child pornography, I would support such a bill. I would wish that the bill would ban *all* pornography, but I would view banning child pornography as a partial victory. But if the leadership of the legislature came to me and said, "Mike, if we pass your child pornography bill, we want your promise that you will never bring up a bill banning adult pornography" —that would be an unacceptable compromise of principle.

Likewise, your boss may say, "We won't require you to go to this seminar on eastern meditation if you'll stop scrutinizing everyone's expense vouchers. You're making us all look bad." You cannot agree to such a compromise if it will mean promising to close your eyes to dishonesty and fraud.

Generally any solution to a problem that moves in the right direction is a partial victory. And if you are free to continue to work for a greater degree of victory in the days and years to come, then take the partial victory and keep working. But if you have to promise to stop your efforts with a less than ideal solution, don't do it. It's all right to seize the "promised land" little by little. But it is not acceptable to seize only half the land and sign a permanent peace treaty ratifying the compromise agreement.

9. *Know how and when to form coalitions.*

If we limit our efforts in our neighborhoods, communities, states, and nation to working only with those groups with whom we have total theological agreement, we are never going to get anything accomplished.

I've worked with all kinds of people over the years that I have absolutely nothing in common with from a theological perspective. My "all time record" in this connection was a man who wanted to support a pro-life effort I was leading, even though he believed in reincarnation. He felt it was grossly unfair for a being to work its way from bug to small animal to horse to human, only to be aborted after the end of a process that took centuries! Obviously I was not going to make this guy a leader on my committee, but I was glad to hand him a piece of literature that identified pro-life candidates so he could vote for them.

There is a major difference between a "coalition" and a permanent organization. A coalition is a group of people who get together on a short-term or temporary basis to try to accomplish a specific effort. If you are trying to remove a New Age indoctrination program from your school, it is a good idea to form a coalition with anyone who supports this goal. You will find Mormons, Catholics, Baptists, and Charismatics all willing to work together on this project. This same group would not be willing to work together to host a seminar on the gifts of the Holy Spirit, but they are only forming a coalition, not a permanent organization.

If your association with a group of people requires you to promise to support these people in future projects, you shouldn't sign up unless the organization is based on a strong biblical foundation. Otherwise you might find yourself being forced to support something you find very wrong.

It's also my experience that you need not be afraid to gather support from groups you normally oppose. If you can get the ACLU *and* the National Association of Evangelicals to both support your position, go for it. Remember we stand for principles, not personalities. Anything you join should have a statement of principle as its foundation.

Be willing to work with a variety of people. Coalition building is a weapon that works.

10. *Persistence pays.*

When I was in Washington State lobbying for a Christian organization, we put on a major push to stop state-funded abortions. We were very close to accomplishing this aim. The decision was coming down to a few votes in the state senate. We put on a major phone campaign to get calls and letters to senators from their home district. The Senate majority leader was a Republican woman from a very conservative part of the state. She was also a professing Christian. There were a number of churches in her district that put on major efforts to call this senator. Her office received over 2,000 calls on this issue.

But she had been put into her position as majority leader by liberal Republicans from the Seattle area. They called in the political favors she owed them and she cast her deciding vote in favor of abortion funding. The people in her district were furious.

But we had a bill coming up a few weeks later on pornography. This time the senator knew she couldn't cross her constituents a second time. She literally rammed the bill that I wrote through the Senate. It was passed and became law. (And was eventually approved by the United States Supreme Court with the exception of one word.)

Let me tell you that there was a strong temptation to burn all of our bridges with this senator when she voted the wrong way on the abortion funding bill. And we did let her know we were not happy in the least. But we stopped short of burning the bridges. She knew she had to help in some meaningful way to buy back some semblance of favor from the 2,000 people who were mad at her.

Be persistent. If persistence requires you to go back to your school board for five years in a row to accomplish something, keep going back. If persistence requires you to keep working on people who have just violated a campaign promise, keep working. (You also need to work to find a new candidate at the next election, but in the meantime don't give up.) Persistence may require you to keep appealing up a chain of command for four or five different levels until you reach someone who agrees with you.

Persistence almost always pays, at least in the long run. You may not win the issue you are concerned about today, but your faithful persistence may be the key to winning some later issue coming before the same decision maker. Remember the parable of the unjust judge and the persistent widow in Luke 18. She kept coming back and coming back. Finally, the judge gave in to her demand for justice. Politics haven't changed much in 2,000 years. Persistence is a weapon that works.

Now that we have surveyed our best tactics, let's examine one of the most pressing issues of the day—public education. The battle for America's children is indeed a fight, and we'll see how to put these weapons to good use.

◊ **4** ◊

The Battle Over Public Education

Joe Johnson sat down at the breakfast table with his morning coffee and newspaper. A headline grabbed his attention; he felt a sinking feeling in his stomach. "First graders to view positive gay lifestyles."

That is the headline that greeted parents in the Bay Ridge district of Brooklyn recently. The Department of Education directed the local school district to teach the first-grade students "to acknowledge the positive aspects of gay and lesbian households." Even though the local superintendent objected to this program, the department held firm—especially in light of the demands of the Lesbian and Gay Teachers Association. A leader of this association declared that the need for this program was predicated on a determination that the old curriculum was wrong. He said, "The children were getting messages that their gay or lesbian families were somehow wrong. I think that's immoral."

Joe Johnson laid aside his paper that morning, in turmoil about his own child. "When did this all happen? How come I wasn't informed?" He felt angry and frustrated.

How would you draw the line if your six-year-old child was a first grader in this district? What would you do?*

---

*The names used in all case studies are fictitious, so as to protect identities. This case study is concluded at the end of the chapter.

———

Most parents of elementary-aged children went to school in the 1950s and 1960s. Back then, Christian parents looked at the public schools with overwhelmingly supportive and positive attitudes. Children went to school to learn academics in a clean, disciplined, and safe environment. Today Christian parents look at the public schools with increasing concern and alarm. If you are a parent of school-aged children, you have undoubtedly asked yourself, "What's really going on in the schools? What can I do to protect my children?"

To answer that far-reaching question, I would like to illustrate with several case histories from my practice.

In October 1991, Lori Aldheizer heard an astonishing story from her second-grade son. He came home from the public school he attended in Fort Mill, South Carolina, and told his mother about a program involving a puppet named "Pumsy." Pumsy is a dragon, and the ostensible purpose for Pumsy is to teach children methods for behavior. Children are told that when they are being naughty they are using their "mud mind." When they are excited and playful they are using their "sparkle mind." And when they are calm and thoughtful they are using their "clear mind." Children are also told that they have a pond of crystal clear water inside their heads. Pumsy the Dragon lives in this pond, and Pumsy can help the children gain their clear mind when they need it.

In accordance with the curriculum, the school's guidance counselor teaches this program, and its official name is *Pumsy in Pursuit of Excellence,* published by Timberline Press from Eugene, Oregon. The guidance counselor told Mrs. Aldheizer's son (and the rest of his class) that their mother and father will leave them someday, and "even Jesus and God will leave" them, but Pumsy the Dragon will never leave them. Pumsy is always there to guide their minds and spirits.

Mrs. Aldheizer was stunned. In the middle of the Bible

belt, a public school was engaged in a transparent effort to indoctrinate her child into New Age thinking, complete with a neat little trick that could open him up to a spirit guide.

Her first action was to protect her own child. Quickly, she found a good curriculum and began home schooling her son. She would not return her child to a school that permitted a program that appears to be straight out of New Age manuals.

She also called me for advice on how to handle this situation. I encouraged her to take the first step of gathering as much information as possible from other parents before the school district began to put its "spin" on the situation. As she began to compare notes with other parents, more of the story surfaced. Children had been told that this was a special secret that they should not share with their parents. Some children immediately burst into tears when their parents asked them to explain who Pumsy was. One girl told her mother that she could not be disciplined because she was in her "clear mind" now and her mother had no authority over her clear mind. Who had told her this?

The guidance counselor met with Mrs. Aldheizer and a few other parents. She assured them that this was no New Age program. She claimed to be a born-again Christian, and disclaimed any knowledge of meditation or similar occultic practices. Upon further investigation it was discovered that the counselor was a member of the Unity Church, noted for its New Age tendencies and commitments. Other claims by the counselor were also discovered to be false.

Today, Lori Aldheizer has two concerns, first for her own children and then for the spiritual safety of the children of her friends and neighbors who remain in the public school. Lori is standing tall for both her children and others. She has drawn the line. It is yet too early to tell how this story will end.

Please don't think that this is just happening in South Carolina. I recently told Lori's story to an audience in Canton, Ohio. The next day I got a call from an alarmed mother in a neighboring town. Her son was also being taught by Pumsy the Dragon. A few days later I read a letter to the editor in my local newspaper indicating that this program was here in a school in my own county in northern Virginia.

This *is* a national program and a national problem. And the New Agers and humanists are smart enough not to put all their eggs in one basket. There are a number of other blatant New Age programs alive and well in the public schools. *Bright Beginnings,* by Timberline Press, is a new program especially for a younger age group. A similar program is called DUSO (Developing an Understanding of Self and Others), which features a character called Duso the Dolphin. Anne Marie Morgan of the *Virginia Citizen* magazine wrote:[1]

> Activities used in the Pumsy and DUSO programs bear more than a passing resemblance to New Age *channeling.* Although the objectives may point to "stress management" or enhancing "self-esteem," it is clear that the methods of achieving relaxation, altering mental states or consciousness through mental imaging, and meeting/ consulting with an identifiable being (inner/spirit guides) are all practices associated with Eastern mysticism for thousands of years.
>
> As New Age activist Dick Sutphin pointed out, *"One of the biggest advantages we have as New Agers is, once the occult, metaphysical, and New Age terminology is removed, we have concepts and techniques that are very acceptable to the general public. So we can change the names. . . . In so doing, we can open the door to millions who normally would not be receptive."* [2]

I do not want to diminish the value of prayer in a situation like this. Yet the very week Lori was working on freeing her school district from this program was the week the Supreme Court heard arguments in the *Lee* v. *Wiseman* case on prayer at a middle-school graduation. Christian organizations and ministries donated tens of thousands of dollars to help on this case, which could be very important. But the lawyers on the case did not even argue that daily prayer in the classroom was constitutional. In fact, I was in the Supreme Court when the lawyers for our side openly stated that they felt that

---

[1] *Virginia Citizen.* Fall 1991, p. 3.
[2] "Infiltrating the New Age into Society," *What Is* (Summer 1986).

prayer in the classroom was unconstitutional. So, while we are devoting our time and energy to one very neutral prayer at a graduation exercise, the New Agers are actively at work at a daily program indoctrinating children to use their "spirit guide" sensitizer, Pumsy.

If your children are in the public schools, you must be alert to potentially dangerous programs like *Pumsy in Pursuit of Excellence* and other New Age or humanistic programs. It is very important that on a daily basis you ask your children to tell you what they did in school that day. A good question to ask is: "Did you do anything new or unusual in school today?" Regular visits with your child's teacher can also pay dividends. Ask what they are studying in every area of curriculum. Be sure to ask if there are any other school personnel who are teaching the children. Ask what role the guidance counselor is taking with your child or the class as a whole.

One thing that should serve as an automatic red flag is any program or teacher who tells your child to keep anything a secret from you, the child's parent. Before each school year, sit down with your child and explain the dangerous potential of an adult who might seek to manipulate a child with the idea of keeping something "secret" from his or her parents. This is the gimmick that sexual child abusers use for their victims. Tell your child that any adult who tries to get them to keep a secret from you may be dangerous and try to harm them. They should report any such incident to you immediately.

When children share their school activities with their parents, not only can they find protection from New Age or humanistic indoctrination, but they may be able to alert their parents to important opportunities to protect our religious heritage and religious freedom.

It is important to stand up for the right of honoring our nation's Christian heritage in the public schools. In fact, the very first public school issue I ever undertook was an attempt to reverse the Spokane Public School District's ban on Christ in school Christmas celebrations. With the help of the pastor of a large Assembly of God Church, we gathered over a thousand people in a city park to stand on a freezing Sunday afternoon in December in protest of this decision. Our collective voice caused the school district to retreat.

And I brought a federal lawsuit on the same issue in a much warmer climate a few years later when a school district near Orlando decided to ban Christmas with a vengeance. Jill Reichert was in a Christmas art contest in her middle school. She drew a nativity scene to adorn the front door of her classroom. Out of all the door decorations in the whole school, hers was the only nativity scene. Her teacher made her tear it down, citing the "separation of church and state."

In a neighboring elementary school, Olivia Meyers was confronted by her teacher for handing out stickers to all her classmates. Olivia was participating in a class project where each child brought a treat one day to celebrate the holidays. When it was Olivia's turn, rather than buying candy, she bought stickers for all the children. The problem was that Olivia's stickers said "Smile God loves you." The teacher confiscated the stickers and took them to the principal who confirmed that Olivia's stickers were "unconstitutional."

Eventually, the school district learned its lesson. They apologized to Olivia and Jill. And they paid them a few thousand dollars each for violating their civil rights. As a result of the lawsuit and a rally held by local churches, the school even reversed its ban on *Silent Night*, which had been removed from the selections to be sung by a school choir.

It is not unconstitutional for your child to engage in religious speech, personal prayer, or to use a religious theme in an art or writing project. Your children should be informed that they have these rights. And if you learn of a violation of these rights, you can take steps of action we outline throughout this book to protect your children's religious freedom.

These small battles are important but the real battle that matters most in public schools is over curriculum. Humanists and New Agers want the opportunity to demean Christianity and to promote their own religious values.

The first curriculum case I entered was in Mead, Washington, a suburb of Spokane. In that case the school district required tenth-grade students to read a book called *The Learning Tree* by Gordon Parks. This book severely demeans

Christianity, Christians, and even goes so far as to call Jesus Christ a "long-legged white s— of a b—." And there were no "blanks" left in this public school textbook.

Carolyn Grove was incensed that her daughter Cassie would be forced to read such a book. She complained and the teacher assigned her an alternative. But she was forced to sit in class and listen while the class discussed the book. The teacher made fun of Cassie for refusing to read this text, which also depicted sexual misconduct and foul language. Carolyn rightfully believed that if it was unconstitutional to have Bible reading in the public school, then it was unconstitutional to denigrate Jesus Christ in the public school class her daughter attended.

She took her complaint to the principal. He appointed a committee that was full of representatives from the teacher's union and the administration. They rubber-stamped the decision to use the text. An appeal to the school board followed. Another rubber stamp. We sued in federal district court. We lost. We appealed to the Ninth Circuit Court of Appeals. Another loss. We appealed to the United States Supreme Court. Appeal was denied without hearing.

Parents who desire to remove curriculum from the public schools need to learn the lesson of *Grove* v. *Mead School District.* Just because a book attacks Christianity or promotes the religion of secular humanism, do not expect any help from the courts. They are blind to the common-sense arguments that it is unfair to throw out any program that remotely promotes Christianity, while approving programs that attack Christianity.

While this was bad, we always had the fall-back option whereby a parent could "opt out" of offensive material and have their children receive alternative instruction. Or so I thought.

Opting Out Tested in Tennessee

My assumption about opting out was tested in Church Hill, Tennessee, in 1983. Vicki Frost, whom I mentioned in Chapter 2, is a mother with incredible courage and tenacity.

She discovered that her children's new reading series contained some unusual ideas and stories. These stories promoted humanism, a one-world government, the occult, the portrayal of man as God, situation ethics, disobedience to parents, magic, and themes of death.

A national authority on ideological balance in textbooks, Dr. Paul Vitz, a psychology professor from New York University, ultimately conducted an examination of this reading series. He noted that one study contained a scene where a boy disparages his mother for teaching him from the Bible. Jesus was portrayed as being illiterate in another story.

Dr. Vitz summarized his findings as follows:

> Religion [in these books] is exotic and foreign—not something characteristic of ordinary American life today; the "exotic" forms of religion portrayed are attractive and supported by the schools.
>
> The net effect of omitting God, Christianity and Protestantism (especially conservative biblical Protestantism) while portraying alternative religions, occult practices, and hostile secular world views such as feminism, is to create a very strong bias against the religion and religious world view of the [parents].

Vicki Frost took her complaint to the school principal at the middle school first. He was very cordial and agreed to give her two children alternative reading books—the books the school used the previous year. By this time, there were a half dozen families who had become alerted to the problems with the Holt Basic Readers and they also worked out the same arrangement with the principal.

This reading series was not confined to the middle school. When Mrs. Frost tried to work out a similar arrangement for her elementary children, trouble began. The principal of the elementary school wasn't as cooperative. And then the school board got involved. They ruled that under no circumstances would these children be allowed to read a different textbook. In November, the middle school principal was directed to suspend all children who refused to read these books. Marty Frost, Rebecca Frost, Travis Mozert, Steve Whitaker, Gina Marshall, Billy Couch, and James Easton were suspended for thirteen days for refusing to read textbooks their parents found offensive.

On the morning of November 23, 1983, Vicki Frost went to the elementary school to remove her second-grade daughter from reading class. The elementary principal had her arrested. Vicki was taken to jail, fingerprinted, and had her mug shot taken.

She used her "one call" from jail to call me. It was the day before Thanksgiving. Immediately, I called the judge and asked what the charge was. He told me that they were trying to figure that out. I demanded her immediate release and he assured me she would be released "soon"—which meant as soon as they could figure out what to charge her with.

That day began the most controversial set of lawsuits I have ever been involved in. I filed suit in federal district court for a violation of the parents' and students' civil rights for expelling the children from school and for forcing these children to read offensive books. I asked the federal court for a temporary injunction to allow the children to go back to school and read alternative books. My motion was denied.

That same afternoon we went to state court on behalf of Vicki Frost's arrest at the elementary school. I pointed out that the statute they charged her with—"trespassing on school property"—had been ruled unconstitutional by a federal court eleven years earlier, and in any event specifically stated that parents had the right to be on school property. The local judge was under tremendous pressure from the community leaders. Visibly shaken as he took the bench after a recess, he reluctantly dismissed the charges.

The civil rights case went through a tortuous path until we finally reached a full trial in front of Judge Thomas Hull, chief federal judge for the Eastern District of Tennessee. The official case name, *Mozert* v. *Hawkins County Public Schools,* was dubbed by the media as the *Scopes II* case. The trial was attended by a glut of media, not only from all over America but from Europe as well.

Nine attorneys opposed me: The local county attorney who never spoke in court; two lawyers for the school district's insurance company; the lawyer for the Tennessee branch of the National Education Association; the chief deputy Attorney General and an assistant attorney general; and three high-priced lawyers from the Washington, D.C., firm of Wilmer, Cutler, and Pickering, who were furnished by the People for the American Way. I was assisted by two lawyers who worked with me at Concerned Women for America who had never participated in a full trial before.

After eight days of grueling trial and media glare, Judge Hull took the case under advisement. To the great shock of all those reading the media accounts—the decision went in our favor. In an exemplary opinion Judge Hull decisively ruled that the school had violated these parents' and students' rights.

But our victory was short-lived. The United States Court of Appeals for the Sixth Circuit heard the appeal and ruled that parents have no right to protect their children from religiously offensive instruction in the public school. The only remedy, the court held, was to exercise the parents' right to home school, or to put their children into a private school.

This case was constitutionally important and made front-page news. I appeared on *Donahue, Nightline, McNeil-Lehrer Report,* ABC News, CBS News, and NBC News. There was a full editorial page on the case in *USA Today*—twice. Everyone expected the United States Supreme Court to take this case on appeal.

To the suprise of lawyers on both sides and the media, the Supreme Court refused to hear the case, without comment. The net effect of this ruling is that parents cannot expect to get any help from the court system in battles to protect their children from ungodly material. Someday I hope there will be a case that will reverse this decision. And it should definitely be reversed. But for now, realism dictates that parents use other means to fight for their children's rights in the public school.

You can probably convince a teacher or principal to allow your child to opt out of any program that violates your beliefs. Even though you may face legal barriers if such a case is brought to court, you probably can win the right to opt out if you quietly appeal to the teacher, the principal, and then on up the chain of command. Your chances of winning the right to opt for your child will be seriously diminished, however, if you focus the issue as an effort to remove the offending material from the school. Any effort that would appear to be "censorship" will meet with much more serious resistance than an effort to simply get your child excused.

Steps of Action You Can Take

I want to share two different kinds of action you can take. The first list focuses on how to deal with individual problems that are short-term matters. The second list addresses long-range solutions to some of the problems facing parents with children in the public school.

Short-Range Steps of Action

1. *Do your homework.* It is easy to walk into a school and claim that a textbook is "unbalanced" or "anti-Christian." If the principal asks, "Have you read the book?"—you will look very silly if the answer is "no." Mel and Norma Gabler have become potent forces for reviewing textbooks in the state of Texas because they meticulously do their homework.

If you have a complaint about a book, read it. If you have a concern about a sex education program, review the plan of instruction. If you have heard that a teacher is condemning Christianity in his class, ask several students to verify the claims and then talk with the teacher before confronting his superiors.

You will never stray too far if you ask questions first and make demands for change later.

2. *Find an ally, if possible.* While you should never be afraid to stand alone, in most public-school issues this is unnecessary. You should do your best to find as many allies as possible for your position.

Let's consider an example of how to find an ally to respond to a proposed sex education curriculum that is unacceptable.

The first place to look for allies is among other parents.

Ask other people in your church who have children in the same school to join with you. Also try to find believers from other churches to help.

In many circumstances you will be able to find an ally inside the school system. If you take the time to call or visit a few people—teachers, principals, administrators—and simply ask questions and seek their opinion before offering yours, you may find an insider who also opposes the sex education program. But if you walk into every office with your guns blazing, potential friends will duck for cover. Listen first and you may find a well-located friend.

You also should try a third source for allies—officials outside the school system. If you know that your mayor is a pro-family advocate, a visit to the mayor to share information about the program and seek his assistance may turn out to be very beneficial. State legislators are also a very good source for outside help in resolving school district problems.

3. *Make reasonable requests.* If you have a dispute about a textbook, don't demand that the book be removed from the entire school system the following day. Instead, ask: "Can you please look into my concerns, and if you find that the book has the failures I have indicated, would you take it to the school board to see if they would remove it from the curriculum?" Your bottom line is still the same—you would like the offending text out, but you have been reasonable in terms of the process to be followed and the time frame.

By the way, if there is a study committee for any issue you're concerned about, it's reasonable to ask that you be on the committee and that the committee be fairly balanced with supporters and opponents.

Another reasonable demand would be, "I believe that this book requiring my child to engage in New Age meditation practices is not proper for my child. I would like to have my child opt out of the program right now while you investigate its suitability for other children."

One sign that you are making a reasonable request is by presenting the school officials with options. This is not always possible, but if you're creative you may be able to construct two or three alternatives that would be acceptable to you.

For example, you could say, "We would either like the sex education course removed from the curriculum or else require its specific contents to be disclosed to all parents. Then those children whose parents affirmatively choose the program should receive instruction. In any event, we would like our children out of the program and they could either take study hall or it would be fine if you could teach them from the sex education program put out by [for example] *Teen Aid.*" Presenting options makes you sound as reasonable as you want to be.

An option that should always be considered is asking to have your child opt out of an offensive program. If your child is given a textbook that you believe is too humanistic or contains New Age or other false philosophies, ask for an alternative text.

Here is an important point about reviewing textbooks. Whenever you want to review a textbook, ask to look at the *teacher's edition* so that you can see the questions the teacher is going to use. Sometimes these questions point out things that are quite revealing of the author's true intentions.

Even though the courts went against us in *Mozert,* you do have a realistic chance of getting an alternative text. If you hit resistance, seek legal help (see Chapter 16). Someday the right case will come forward to allow the courts to reverse this horrible decision.

If your child is being forced to participate in a program that is clearly oriented toward New Age religion, such as Pumsy the Dragon, I believe your chances of legal victory are much stronger than in cases involving humanistic textbooks. Courts have a hard time understanding the religious nature of humanism. Perhaps they will have an easier time understanding why parents do not want their children subjected to the psychotherapy techniques, post-hypnotic suggestions and guided-imagery exercises during classroom time.

Do not threaten a lawsuit during your first meeting unless a lawyer has advised you otherwise. In fact, *never* threaten a lawsuit unless you believe that you have available counsel and the funding. Talk of lawsuits should only come up when there has been an utter breakdown in the process of negotiation of your reasonable demands.

Above all, do not employ a demeanor that sets you up for failure. If you come across as a brash person who is going to insist on winning at all costs, a school official is going to be tempted to want to beat you, simply as a matter of a contest of the wills. Persistence is a good attribute. Boldness is a wonderful characteristic. But when these qualities are joined by humbleness and patience, you have a winning combination.

4. *Even if you face hostility, decide that you will not be intimidated.* Confrontation is not pleasant. If you have come to a principal and asked for his assistance in dealing with a teacher who has ridiculed your child's Christianity, you may occasionally get a response like, "Well, it's good for the kid to face a little ridicule. It toughens him up for real life." That is an effort at intimidation. Don't cave in. Respond to such statements by saying: "I don't appreciate your pressure right now. I really need your help in resolving a serious issue that concerns the well-being of my child."

Don't be afraid of statements like, "You are the only parent who feels this way." It's probably not true, but it is always appropriate to say, "Yes, but I'm the only mother my child has, and I have the responsibility to protect her."

If a person continues to engage in intimidating kinds of statements, leave. And immediately find a higher ranking person to discuss the problem.

5. *Keep appealing.* The general chain of command in most public school districts goes like this: (1) teacher; (2) principal; (3) assistant superintendent; (4) superintendent; (5) school board; (6) state department of education; (7) state board of education. There are many situations for which you cannot get any help at the state level. This is especially true if you're trying to resolve a problem that's unique to your child or a particular teacher. But in most situations you should consider continuing your appeals up the ladder until you either get victory or hit the final wall.

6. *Consider your legal options.* Schools can be sued and sometimes should be sued for their mistreatment of students or their infringement of the rights of parents. Chapter 16 gives

details on legal matters. You should never undertake a law-suit lightly. But you should not hesitate to at least seek a preliminary opinion if you believe that either you or your child has been denied your rights or have been dealt with improperly or illegally.

Long-Range Steps of Action

1. *Consider your options.* Seriously consider whether or not the public schools are really the place God would have you keep your children for their education. Study the Bible to check out passages where God gives principles on the education of children and see if you should make a switch to Christian education in your own home or in a local Christian school. It is definitely important to battle for good public schools, but you may not want your own children caught in the cross-fire while the battle is raging.

2. *Focus on your school board.* Most issues of concern to Christian parents will be resolved by local school boards. You need to be ready to appeal adverse decisions to the local school board. Even though the federal courts have ruled that schools don't have to give your children alternative books or allow them to opt out, it's been my experience that most school boards will allow opt-out options and alternative instruction. You can win on the local political level what you may not be able to win in the legal arena.

Elect good parent-oriented school board members. School board members who merely "rubber stamp" administration decisions should be defeated at the next election. This is one of the easiest elections in America to influence. Organize a group and run a slate of candidates. Good school board members can make a substantial difference. You may want to consider this office yourself.

3. *Pay special attention to any program of sex education or so-called "family life education."* Demand to see the actual textbooks and teacher's editions in advance of the adoption of any program. If your state legislature is considering mandatory sex education—*you had better fight that bill then and there.* Don't wait until it is voted into law and then go after your local school board: It's too late for that.

If your child is placed in a sex education course, you can ask for her to be excused. (I do not believe that there are very many sex education courses in the entire country that Christian students should be exposed to.) The only exception is a course published by a group called Teen Aid from Spokane, Washington. It is available nationally, but is rarely adopted by the public schools.

4. *Become informed on the legally permissible role of religion in the public schools.* If your child engages in student-initiated religious activity, it is unconstitutional for school officials to interfere. If your child wants to pray over his lunch, school officials cannot stop him, though they may try. If your child wants to write a paper, draw a picture, or make a speech that refers to Christianity or the Bible, his efforts cannot be censored simply because of their religious content as long as he stays within the general assignment. For example, if your child is asked to give a speech on ethics in politics, he is free to refer to the Bible as the proper source for ethics.

Concerned Women for America has a very helpful booklet on the legal rules for Christmas celebrations in the public schools. They also provide legal assistance in this arena. Jay Sekulow leads an excellent organization called Christian Advocates Serving Evangelism (CASE), which provides legal help for students desiring to exercise their religious freedom in the public schools. Christian Legal Society also provides good publications, information, and assistance in this area as well. See the Appendix for address information for these organizations.

One of the most important developments in the public schools has been the advent of the Equal Access Act. Congress enacted this law to permit religious student organizations to have the same rights as any other student organization. Christian Legal Society took the lead in getting this bill through Congress, but were aided by a number of other organizations. If your child desires to have a Bible study or other Christian student activity or club on campus, contact Christian Legal Society, CWA, or CASE for the exact parameters of this law. The United States Supreme Court has already heard a challenge to this law and upheld it as constitutional. Thousands of student clubs are now meeting regularly in the public schools thanks to this excellent legislation.

5. *Advocate a long-range solution to our educational crisis.* I believe that America will continue to have low academics and low morality in the schools until each and every school becomes parent-controlled. In essence, the very best system of school government would be to have the parents of each school elect a school board to govern that one school. Then that board and the principal could run the school in a proper and more economically feasible manner.

There are tens of thousands of administrators all over the nation collecting billions in salaries who never teach a child. The enormous waste we have from national, state, and local departments of education is a serious drain on our national resources and does not result in any real advances for academic education of children.

Parent control of education works. When parents are involved, silly and dangerous experiments on the lives of their children will be avoided.

Steps of Action for Drawing the Line

Joe Johnson and other parents in Bay Ridge, New York, need to take action to reverse the policy that will force first graders to listen to so-called positive aspects of gay and lesbian lifestyles.

It is significant that the local superintendent is on the right side of the issue. Parents need to rally to his support. If this superintendent tries to face down the Department of Education alone, his job will be much more difficult. In fact, his employment may be on the line if he goes too far. Joe and other parents need to support and work closely with this man.

Parents should get permission to use a school building for an "informational meeting," which should be used to rally support against this program. They can begin gathering signatures from the community; then they should call state legislators from their area whose vote on funding for the public schools is important to school board members.

They should contact a lawyer to see if this sex education program may be illegal. Most states have a law on the books that requires all instruction to be morally upright. This is a seldom-enforced law, but can be a good weapon. In many states, homosexual activity (sodomy) is still a crime. If this is the case, then there is a good argument that teaching children how to engage in criminal conduct is legally impermissible.

The linchpin of the strategy should be focused on the Department of Education, which made the decision in the first place. The phone should not stop ringing and their mailbox should be full.

Ultimately, if the department does not succumb to this kind of community outcry, parents need to remove their child from school whenever such instruction is offered. If enough people opt out, the department will see that they have a real mess on their hands and will be forced to pull the program. If opt out is not permitted, parents should consider opting out of the school system entirely.

A Final Note: The Long-Term Battle

In 1981, I defended Suzanne Clark, a mother from Bristol, Tennessee, who had written a letter to the editor of her local newspaper concerning the National Education Association. The NEA sued Suzanne for claiming that the organization was promoting secular humanism. Our defense? Her letter told the truth.

In the course of that lawsuit, we were able to take the depositions of the highest officials of the NEA. We had access to a number of their internal files and documents. The long-range nature of the battle we face over public education is evidenced by the information I discovered in that case. The NEA dropped its suit, because it appeared that we would prevail in our effort to prove their humanistic bent. They did change their minds about suing Suzanne Clark—but not on their adherence to humanistic principles.

The NEA is more than an organization. Its official policies represent a world view that cannot possibly be reconciled with biblical Christianity. The vast majority of the education establishment holds to the same world view whether or not they are officially members of the NEA.

In 1981, I became convinced that the education establishment rejects the Judeo-Christian moral absolutes upon which our nation was founded. They believe that children should be brought up into a self-directed, not God-directed, way of thinking. The situation has not gotten better in the last decade; rather, it has clearly deteriorated. The open use of New Age activities is worse today than it was in the early 1980s.

Even if you choose to educate your children at home or in a Christian school—which we will discuss in the next chapter—as taxpayers and voters, we need to be concerned about the fate of the millions of children who will remain in the public schools.

The battle will not be easy, because both sides recognize that the stakes are all-important—the hearts and minds of the next generation. We need to protect our own children and their right to receive an education that is consistent with their Christian heritage.

The Battle for Private Education: Christian and Home Schools

Pastor James Stobaugh and his wife, Karen, decided that the best educational plan for their family was to teach them at home. They did not believe that the Pittsburgh public schools could provide the kind of academic education they desired for their children—that is, an education based on Christian principles. The first thing many people asked them about home schooling was: Is that legal?

The question had been up in the air for a long time in Pennsylvania. At that time in 1987, I had more home-school cases in court pending in Pennsylvania than in any other state. On behalf of a number of families, I filed a statewide federal civil rights lawsuit challenging the constitutionality of the old state law.

The Stobaughs joined in rejoicing with other home-schooling families in Pennsylvania in 1988 when a federal court declared their state's home-schooling law unconstitutional. That law gave each local superintendent the unbridled discretion to control home education as he saw fit. The rejoicing was especially enthusiastic in Pittsburgh because that city's superintendent was well known for his tough policies and severe restrictions.

The Pennsylvania legislature passed a new and far more lenient law to replace the previous unconstitutional statute. The Stobaughs rejoiced again.

While the rest of the state became peaceful, though, the celebration in Pittsburgh was definitely premature. The superintendent sent James and Karen and other home-schooling families letters informing them that they could expect school officials to appear at their door for a "home visit." They were also informed that they would be required to have their children take a series of public school tests *over and above* the testing required by the new law. In some grades, up to 17 tests were required in a single year. The Stobaughs could expect no fewer than a dozen tests for their children, Rachel and Jessica.

Both the "home visit" requirement and the testing requirement were clearly in excess of what state law required. But when the Stobaughs and other families informed the superintendent that they were sticking by what the law required, he began the steps to revoke James and Karen's right to home school their children.

How should the Stobaughs and other families respond?

―――――

Many of the greatest battles for religious freedom have been fought over education. The public schools have been the battleground for America's most strident debates over the Establishment of Religion Clause (the so-called separation of church and state). Christian schools and home schools have been on the front lines for the battle to preserve the free exercise of religion.

Some of the confrontations facing those desiring to give their children a Christian education have been:

- Local officials who appear at home-schooling parents' front door demanding that the children be immediately enrolled in the public schools.
- Christian schools that have been harassed in some states so severely that police officials have padlocked churches and arrested pastors and jailed parents.
- Efforts to require parents to possess a teaching certificate in order to home school their children. This would ban 98 percent of parents who desire to teach their own

children despite statistical proof that uncertified parents can teach just as well.

- Misuse of zoning laws to stop churches from starting new Christian schools in their existing buildings—even though the buildings are properly zoned as churches.

Life is full of ironies—but no irony has been greater in my own life than the fact that I've spent the majority of my legal career in court litigating against public school officials. I have spent more than a decade defending home schools, Christian schools, and Christian parents in conflict with the public schools. Here is the irony: My father was a public school principal, and my initial career plan was to become a lawyer who defended school districts! My undergraduate honors thesis was written on the topic of school law. I was trained by a professor who was also a lawyer for the Washington State School Boards Association. If I'd kept on that career path, I would have had a good chance at a prominent and lucrative career representing school officials.

My original motivation came from my father. He convinced me that school districts needed to be defended from attacks by the ACLU and other liberal organizations. But by the time I got through school, by and large, those who ran the schools were *sympathetic* to the aims of the ACLU. Like my father, I know that there are many dedicated Christians who are teachers and administrators in the public schools. But they are increasingly on the defensive and in the minority.

When our oldest child reached school age, my wife, Vickie, and I decided that we should give our daughter a Christian education. Because of my family background, this was not an easy decision. But we could not ignore the information we'd obtained as a result of my work and research in school law and my wife's training in education courses. We knew that the humanistic philosophy was just too prevalent in our school system. Eventually, we chose home schooling.

The home-schooling movement captured headlines in the 1980s and into the 1990s. Today, between 500,000 and 700,000 children are being taught by their parents at home.

To the dismay of many home-schooling families, however, the humanists who control the public schools also control the legal mechanisms that regulate private education. Often it seems that those regulators go out of their way to make life difficult for those of us seeking an alternative to the public schools. Some, in fact, have paid a great price for the freedom to pursue private education.

Seven Brave Dads

I'll never forget seven fathers from Louisville, Nebraska, who sat in a county jail for 93 days because they dared to send their children to a Christian school. It was their courageous battle that marked a turning point in the battle for freedom of Christian schools.

Faith Baptist Church in Louisville had been through a long legal confrontation. Their case had already been to the Supreme Court of Nebraska, which had ordered the school closed. The pastor of the church had been in and out of jail a number of times. But the parents persisted in sending their children to the only Christian school in town, convinced that the court's decision had been in error—both legally and spiritually. In order to stop this school, the sheriff even carried out a raid on a church worship service. (We will discuss this in detail in Chapter 11.)

I was not involved in the early stages of this case, but I began working on it as a civil rights lawsuit against the sheriff for conducting the raid on the worship service. Frankly, I disagreed with some of the tactics of the pastor and a few of the outside leaders who came in to help. A few exhibited an attitude of rebellion that did nothing but hurt the cause. It was clear to me, however, that the majority of those who came to help were honorable, decent, and wise Christians. Pastor Bob McCurry from Atlanta was exemplary in the face of very difficult circumstances. But it was not outside pastors who were facing the real difficulties—it was the parents whose children were attending the church school in Faith Baptist Church.

On November 23, 1983, seven fathers were hauled into

court for sending their children to this Christian school. When these fathers invoked their Fifth Amendment right to remain silent, the judge threw them in jail—the day before Thanksgiving.

A legal battle followed, on several fronts—the Nebraska Supreme Court, federal district court, and even the United States Supreme Court. The fate of these seven men was most definitely on the front burner of legal and political issues.

These men were jailed in deplorable conditions. While burglars and thieves were allowed to go outside to shovel snow for exercise, these "dangerous" Christian fathers were strictly confined to their cells. Yet they continually responded with positive spirits and attitudes, despite the fact that they spent Christmas in jail, missed children's birthdays, and many lost their jobs. Eventually, their quiet courage prevailed. The governor appointed a task force, which concluded the fathers were right, and that it was a violation of constitutional rights to forcibly close this Christian school and impose excessive state regulation. Reluctantly, the judge released these men from jail after this committee had begun its process, and it appeared serious about protecting the rights of these fathers.

The legal battles faced by Christian schools have been toned down, but not have gone away. I believe there are two reasons for this. One, the courage of these seven fathers has helped to break the willingness of the legal system to do the bidding of the humanist educators. A national Christian school leader told me the second reason: Since the homeschooling movement has come to the forefront, the legal battles have shifted. Christian schools are still attacked, but the battle for the right to home school has helped to divert much of our opponents' manpower.

There are four "fronts" on which we continually face opposition to Christian and home-school freedoms:

Lines of Conflict

1. *State control of teachers.*
Most home-school and Christian-school battles have been

fought over efforts of regulators to specify who will be permitted to teach children. This was the situation in Nebraska. The regulators demanded that the school employ only those licensed by the government, that is, state-certified teachers. The Christian school wanted to employ teachers with college degrees, but refused on principle to obtain licenses from the government.

In many states, in order to become a state-certified teacher it is necessary to take courses in humanistic psychology and other practices clearly contrary to Christian values. While it might appear the issue is quality, the real issue is control.

Scripture makes it clear that it is the responsibility of parents to direct the education of their children (Deuteronomy 4:9–10; 11:18–21).

My first concern for any person who would teach my children is their spiritual condition. I am also concerned that my children receive good academic instruction, but the evidence is clear that we need not sacrifice spiritual qualifications for academic excellence. Study after study has demonstrated that certified teachers perform no better than other people in terms of being able to teach children. I have a doctorate in law and an undergraduate degree in political science. I have the qualifications to teach in any university or law school. But I would not be permitted to teach a basic government course at any public high school because I am not "certified" to teach. A teacher's certification law sounds plausible until you look at the evidence. This is particularly true with home schooling. Students who are taught by parents without a teaching certificate, and even without a college degree, perform much higher than public school students.

One of the reasons teacher's certification laws make no sense is the nature of teacher education in this country. My wife has a degree in elementary education and was a certified teacher—yet she was never taught how to teach phonics. She was taught values clarification and humanistic psychology. But she was not taught how to properly teach reading.

If you want to give children an opportunity to learn and become spiritually mature, possessing a license from the state is an irrelevancy.

Fortunately, teacher's certification is becoming a legal irrelevancy as well. Thanks to the courageous stand of the seven fathers and the good report of the governor's task force, the Nebraska legislature changed the law. No longer are Nebraska home schools or Christian schools required to use state-certified teachers.

The most notorious battle over teacher's certification for home schoolers was fought in North Dakota. Family after family was prosecuted for teaching their own children without possessing a state teaching certificate. The regulators and prosecutors simply did not care that the children were learning.

In Mandan, North Dakota, the prosecutor subpoenaed eight-year-old Carrie Dagley to testify against her parents. I was able to protect her from this, but it was a troubling experience. Each month there was a new case in court.

Finally, we hit upon a strategy that began to pay political dividends. A number of home schoolers came from all over America to stand with our persecuted brothers and sisters. On the plane flying to Bismarck, I began thinking about our nation's history and our commitment to freedom. I kept ruminating on what one of my daughters had asked me: "Why can't they home school in North Dakota? This is a free country, isn't it?"

When I spoke to the rally that night, my theme was "The Consent of the Governed." I challenged the crowd to help me teach the North Dakota legislature a basic lesson in freedom. We went to K-Mart and bought every tea bag in the store. And on the bags we stapled a little card that read "Bismarck Tea Party" and "Consent of the Governed for Home Schoolers." The next day every person in the capital was handed at least one tea bag. The media picked up the theme of the Bismarck Tea Party. A few days later, the legislature finally ended the three-year struggle when they repealed the law requiring parents to be certified teachers.

Only Michigan has kept its law requiring certified teachers for all private schools and home schools. But a few other states have erected other barriers to prevent parents from being allowed to teach their own children. One-by-one these barriers are being challenged, and I believe these will eventually fall.

2. *Misuse of zoning laws and building codes.*

When Romania was under the Communists, a church asked for permission to expand their building. Permission was repeatedly denied. Finally, in frustration, the church built the addition anyway. The government sent bulldozers to level the church building. The church was charged with violating zoning laws.

Zoning laws are also at work in America to limit the freedom of churches. This is particularly true when it comes to the issue of Christian schools.

Churches have been told:

- On Sunday (for church), classroom doors may swing to the inside; on Monday (for school), they must swing to the outside.
- For church, the building must be 30 feet from the property line. For school, the building must be 40 feet from the property line.
- On Sunday, the church building is safe for 1,000. On Monday it is safe for only 250.

It is difficult to move a church building back and forth after Sunday evening services. Zoning and building laws for churches and schools have historically developed on two tracks. It is often a pragmatic impossibility for one building to meet both sets of standards—although in terms of public safety if the building meets either standard, safety is ensured.

In Tacoma, Washington, a new independent charismatic church bought the building formerly occupied by an old mainline church that had simply died away. The church fully met all building and zoning requirements for its use as a church. But when the church decided to operate a Christian school, city officials told them they would have to get their building rezoned for the additional use as a school. They applied, and then the city denied them the right to have a school.

They brought the problem to me. I carefully read the city

zoning ordinance. It was apparent to me that there was no need for the church to have to obtain a second zoning permit. If a building was properly zoned as a church, it was allowed to conduct a school as a matter of right.

The church started the school and was immediately challenged in court by the city. After hearing all of the evidence, the judge ruled that if the principles of religious freedom were applied to the zoning ordinance, it was unnecessary for a church to get new zoning permission every time it started a new ministry.

Zoning is a neutral law that can be used as an effective weapon against Christian schools in the hands of unfriendly bureaucrats. There are many instances where it is obvious that there is no legitimate reason to stop a Christian school, but officials use a zoning law as a barrier. If a building is safe enough and properly zoned to have Sunday school on Sunday, there is no legitimate reason it is not safe enough to have a Christian school on Monday.

Churches would be well-advised, when applying for any zoning or building permit for the initial church building, to specify that someday they may want to conduct a day school in the same facility. This will prevent officials from requiring the church to go through a second process to get one building zoned twice. A second zoning process will be expensive, and it may result in the denial of the right to conduct a Christian school.

3. *Excessive regulation.*

When I started defending home-schooling parents in 1982, the government's position was simple: Home schooling is illegal. We have won that war. Only Michigan still has a law on the books that purports to make home schooling illegal for most parents. And there are still some significant "parent qualification" hurdles in Tennessee and South Carolina. But the regulators haven't given up elsewhere. They want to make home schooling as difficult as possible so that families will give up and put their children back into the public schools. Their current weapon is excessive regulation.

- Some officials have demanded that home schoolers

submit an entire year's lesson plans in advance.

No public-school teacher does this. In fact, it would be educational malpractice to be so rigid in planning that you do not modify your program in light of the needs of your students and their rate of progress.

- Some states have demanded that home-schooling *parents* be tested in order to teach their children at home.

There have been numerous legal battles in South Carolina over this issue. The law requires the parents to be high school graduates and pass a basic literacy test. I keep asking the public school officials one question: If you had any doubt as to the basic literacy of these parents, why did you award them a high school diploma? We recently won a major victory in the Supreme Court of South Carolina, which declared that the program of testing parents in that state was illegal.

- Some states demand that home-schooled children be brought to the public school for testing, using tests specially selected to match public school curriculum.

Most Christian home schoolers periodically give their children a standardized achievement test. But the public schools use testing as another means of making life difficult for home schoolers. It is well known that children test most accurately in their normal learning environment. It is also well known that public schools choose achievement tests to most closely pattern their own curriculum. It is unfair to require home schoolers to use the public school's choice of test when another nationally normed, standardized test might more accurately assess the home-schooled child's course of study. If testing is going to be required, parents should be allowed to choose any nationally recognized test and have it administered by any qualified person of their own choosing. Regulators use control of testing conditions as a fear tactic rather than a legitimate assessment device for the benefit of children.

- Officials demand the right to enter a person's home to conduct an inspection of the home school.

This tool of excessive regulation is euphemistically called the "home visit." Public school officials use this tactic to gain entry into your home for the purpose of "evaluating" your education. I view home visits as an unconstitutional invasion of privacy and a violation of the constitutional rule that prohibits government officials from searching your home without a warrant.

A true "visit" occurs when you invite someone to your home as your guest. It is not a "visit" when a government official demands entry to your home to make a determination whether or not you are complying with a law that has criminal penalties. Several courts have agreed with us that public school officials cannot demand entry into your homes without a search warrant.

We have seen real abuses for those families who have permitted home visits. School officials have wanted to take the children alone and quiz them about a wide range of subjects, including questions like: "Do your parents spank you?"

An official cannot demand entry into your home unless it is specifically authorized by state law. Only South Dakota and North Carolina have laws that even arguably permit home visits. And in those two states I believe that these laws are subject to constitutional challenge.

4. *Bad-faith harassment.*

Maggie Smeltzer attended a Pennsylvania public school for her first three years of education. She was not doing very well academically. In fact, her standardized test scores were so low that she was considered "borderline learning-disabled."

Her parents decided that they would like to try home schooling Maggie to see if they could do any better. The school officials were very reluctant but finally granted permission. After two years of home schooling, Maggie's test scores were so high the school district now considered her "gifted and talented."

You would think that the parents would be commended by the public school officials—but just the opposite happened. After receiving those test scores, the officials decided to deny the Smeltzers the right to home school Maggie for the third year. They ruled that since Maggie was now "gifted and talented" she had to return to the public school because her parents were incapable of teaching a gifted and talented child! To back up their decision, they filed criminal charges against Mr. and Mrs. Smeltzer.

The Smeltzers were members of Home School Legal Defense Association and I got their call. I immediately prepared a federal civil rights law suit against the school officials. In an accompanying letter to the superintendent, I told him that the Smeltzers were responsible for so vastly improving Maggie's education that there was no way they were going to let the school district ruin her education again. I gave the superintendent 24 hours to dismiss his criminal charges, or else I would file the federal civil rights lawsuit he received that day by Federal Express. The charges were dismissed.

One additional fact might help explain this story. School districts get additional government money for gifted and talented children.

There are enough cases of bad-faith harassment of home schoolers to keep five full-time lawyers busy at Home School Legal Defense Association. And I know that such harassment continues against Christian schools as well.

Our Real Defender

God *is* our defender.

A few years ago I flew out to Ohio to defend a mother, Robin Spencer, who was facing criminal charges for home schooling. Her superintendent had denied her permission to home school and quickly followed his denial with criminal charges.

Mrs. Spencer sat with me at her backyard picnic table the day before trial to get prepared. As a part of that preparation I asked about her religious beliefs to see if we could legitimately raise First Amendment defenses. It was obvious that she was confused about her relationship with God, but it was equally obvious that she believed in the Bible and wanted to know the Lord. Right there at her picnic table, I led Robin in a prayer to make sure of her salvation. She was very happy, and so was I. I told her that I thought God was going to do something very powerful in her case to prove himself strong in her life.

When I walked into court the next morning, the judge asked the lawyers to come into his chambers, as is often done. He greeted us all and then addressed me. He said, "Mr. Farris, I have just read a recent decision of the Ohio Supreme Court that ruled against home schooling, and I'm going to follow that decision. You are going to lose today in court." He really didn't convey a bad spirit; he simply made up his mind in advance. (I've been in a number of courts where I felt as if the judge had made up his mind in advance, but this was the first time one of them had the honesty to say it out loud.) He also told me that he would allow me to ask whatever legitimate questions I wanted, and to build a record to see if I could get the Ohio Supreme Court to reverse the earlier decision.

I didn't know what to say or do. In light of the bold promise I'd made to Mrs. Spencer the day before, I was really discouraged.

When the trial started, the prosecutor put the superintendent on the stand first. When it came time for me to cross-examine him, a question dropped into my head from nowhere. It was not a particularly good question from a legal perspective, but I asked it anyway.

"Did you get any legal advice before you made the decision to deny Mrs. Spencer the right to home school?" I asked.

He replied, "I didn't talk to any lawyers, but I did talk to some government officials."

"Oh," I replied, "like who?"

"Well, I talked with the judge here, for one," he stated.

"You talked with *this* judge about *this* lady's case before this matter ever came to court?" I inquired.

I looked up at a very red-faced judge, and called for a recess.

We won the case that day. Both Robin Spencer and Mike Farris were shown that they serve a mighty God. A God who is so powerful that He can overturn a decision a judge has made, through ways we would never expect.

I have seen God intervene in case after case on behalf of parents who are desirous of providing their children with a Christ-centered education.

Steps of Action You Can Take

1. *Make plans for legal protection.*

Both Christian schools and home schools face very real prospects of legal problems. You should be prepared with legal protection in advance of any difficulties. Christian schools can find such protection through the major Christian school organizations—Association of Christian Schools International, and American Association of Christian Schools. Home schoolers are welcome to join the organization I lead: Home School Legal Defense Association (HSLDA).

The addresses of all these organizations can be found in the Appendix.

2. *Know your state's law.*

Many legal conflicts arise when school officials try to place demands on home schools or private schools that are in excess of what state law demands. You can obtain a copy of your state law from a local law library. Home schoolers can also obtain a free summary of the law in their state from HSLDA.

3. *Keep good records.*

Christian schools know the need for good academic and attendance records. Home schoolers need to keep careful records of their work, because our approach appears to be so different to outsiders.

Keep copies of all tests and representative samples of your children's daily work. You should either have lesson plans that you retain, or a daily log that you make after-the-fact to record what you accomplished that day. The results of any standardized achievement test scores must also be retained.

4. *Don't live "in hiding."*

Home schoolers are often afraid for this fact to become known. Hiding is a terrible way to live and will not be good for your children. While you may have good reason to avoid unnecessary contact with your local school officials, I would still advise you to "live with your shades up." If you have made steps for legal preparation, just go about your business in a responsible manner and reject the temptation to live an underground life.

5. *Join your state home schooling or Christian school association.*

State organizations are crucial for the success of long-range efforts to improve legislation for private education. Contact the national organizations listed earlier in this chapter for the name and address of the state organization for Christian schools or home schools.

6. *Try to deal with problems in writing.*

Although you should not treat this as an ironclad rule, it is best to try to conduct all dealings between private schools and public school officials in writing. If you have a conversation, send a follow-up letter restating the basic points made by both parties. If you ever find yourself in court, having written proof of what has transpired is invaluable.

7. *Remember God is your protector.*

Don't forget the story of Robin Spencer. There are dozens of similar stories. While it is good to have an available lawyer and be a part of an organization that will stick up for your rights, it is even more important to be a child of the King.

The Stobaughs and other families facing the situation we described at the beginning of the chapter took four steps of action:

1. They contacted the lower level school officials. They indicated in both written and verbal communications that they believed both requirements—home visits

and extra testing—were beyond what was required by state law. At this point the school district decided not to pursue the home-visit issue, but maintained a strong requirement that the tests were mandatory.

2. They contacted the superintendent. Not satisfied with the answer of the assistant, the appeal was registered with the superintendent. He turned them down flat and even took steps of reprisal.

3. They sought legal assistance. At this point in time, HSLDA began to intervene. I called the school district's lawyer to attempt to reason with him. In the vast majority of cases this would have settled the matter. School officials cannot demand more than is required in state law. Most lawyers recognize this. The lawyers representing Pittsburgh schools did not.

4. We filed a federal civil rights lawsuit on behalf of the Stobaughs and three other families. When reason, appeals and negotiation failed, we appealed to a higher authority—the federal courts. In his ruling, the federal judge held that the superintendent had "arbitrarily chosen to flout state law." And with that sentence, the problem was solved.

◇ **6** ◇

The Battle for Parents' Rights

Closely related to schooling issues is the matter of parents' rights. These would include matters of family privacy and discipline, and parental consent in matters concerning their minor children.

Too often, however, Christian parents are finding these rights violated, with frightening implications. Consider the following:

———

Joanne Stevenson's phone rang one morning as she was finishing a load of laundry. On the other end of the line, a female voice said, "I'm Sarah Jones from the Department of Children's Services. We've just received a hotline report that your husband excessively spanks your children. I'm afraid we'll have to come out in a few minutes to examine the children."

Although both she and her husband spanked their children, Joanne knew that her husband was not guilty of such charges. Last evening, when their ten-year-old had continually shouted at them and then refused to do his chores, he had indeed been spanked. She felt that there was nothing to fear. Besides, she reminded herself, the Bible clearly teaches that we should spank our children. She believed that her rights of religious freedom would also protect her.

Should Joanne tell the social worker to come out and make her examination? What would you do?

———

The right of parents to direct the upbringing of their children and to protect their family's privacy was once considered sacrosanct. Yet today, government officials are becoming more and more willing to invade the sanctity of the home and substitute their judgment for that of a child's parents.

Not all "invasions" of the home are as blatant as the social worker who insists on inspecting your children as we have described in the opening case study. There are more subtle invasions of parental rights, some of which have extraordinary impact on your child's beliefs, morals, well-being, and safety.

Did you know that there is a source where your children can obtain R-rated movies without any adult's permission— and even get these movies for free? You may be in one of those communities in which the local public library keeps R-rated movies in stock and will lend them out to *any* person of *any* age with no questions asked.

Although there are individual librarians who steadfastly resist such policies, the official position of the American Library Association adamantly supports the "right" of children to obtain such materials without the parents' knowledge. While they argue their case in terms of a child's freedom, in reality they are arguing for their rights as adults to give your children R-rated movies without your knowledge or permission. They want to substitute their permissive views of parenting for your biblical views.

This same philosophy was the rationale for the incident mentioned in Chapter 1, where the high school girl was dismissed from school to obtain birth control pills without her mother's knowledge or consent. In fact, the school had assured the mother a strict "closed campus" policy was being enforced. Adults with a liberal child-rearing philosophy are all too willing to override our wishes and allow children to obtain birth control pills without our knowledge.

I am sure you know that as bad as this birth control situation is, it is even worse that millions of teenage girls have been given abortions without their parents' knowledge or consent. Although the Supreme Court has begun to show some willingness to reinstate the right of parents to prior knowledge of their daughter's desire to have an abortion, it requires new state legislation and adults who are willing to abide by the law. The adults who run Planned Parenthood are insistent that they have the right to substitute their advice for the parents' when it comes to issues of abortion and birth control. They argue in terms of a child's rights, but in reality adults are making decisions for someone else's child and administering medical care without the parents' knowledge or consent.

Parents at Risk—
The Work of the Child-Abuse Industry

We have dealt so far with adults who want to substitute their child-rearing philosophy for yours, but are willing to do so while the child still lives in your home. Another substantial risk to your parental rights comes from those who are all too willing to *remove* your children from your home— the growing army of social workers who staff government agencies with names like Children's Protective Services, or Department of Children and Youth.

There is a lonely minority of Christians and others with traditional values who work in these agencies. Their jobs are doubly difficult. First, they have to deal with cases of true child abuse, where intervention is fully justified. But they also face the reality that many of their co-workers have philosophies that threaten the rights of Christian parents to raise children in a biblical fashion. While these agencies are totally justified in targeting true abuse, there is no legal or moral justification for the apparent vendetta being waged by many social workers against Christian parents.

Investigating "Every Bruise"

Consider the plight of a family from Colorado who was investigated for child abuse by government social workers. One of their teenaged daughters passed out due to a medical condition, and her mother took her to the hospital for treatment. During the examination, a medical worker noticed a bruise about the size of a half-dollar on the daughter's back. And because of the presence of a single bruise, he called in the social workers for investigation of child abuse.

When the social workers questioned the girl, she said that she couldn't remember for sure how she got the bruise. She stated that she may have bumped herself on a piece of furniture, but that she and her sister sometimes got into fights which may have caused the bruise. That was enough for the social workers to move into high gear. Even though the only statement they had would indicate "sibling abuse," the family was under investigation for child abuse.

I read the report from the social worker, and he had three "complaints" against the family. First, there was the bruise. Second, his report made much of the fact that the parents were teaching their children at home. Finally, he noted that the family was "heavily into Adams City Baptist Church." Obviously, he felt the combination of these three "patterns of behavior" warranted a serious child-abuse investigation.

In an attempt to get these "charges" dropped, I called the attorney for the social services department. I asked why they were wasting taxpayers' money with such a frivolous case— there was no evidence that the bruise was anything other than a bump from normal living. He told me that in their county they investigate every bruise that they become aware of— even if a child just gets a bruise falling off a bike, they investigate.

Although we were able to get this investigation halted, not every Christian family is able to stop these problems so easily. And it's not just bruises that can get you in trouble.

Too Much Church? You Can Lose Your Child!

When I was practicing law in Washington State, I defended a family who was facing charges because they "forced their child to attend church too much"!

The boy in question was about thirteen years old and his mother, who was divorced, had recently become a Christian and remarried a Christian man. The family went to church on Sunday morning, Sunday evening, and Wednesday night for prayer meeting. The boy rebelled, refusing to go to anything more than Sunday morning services.

At his public school he was told by counselors that the law in Washington State allowed him to seek shelter in a foster home if he was having conflict with his parents. He applied for this "protection," and it was immediately granted without any notice to the parents.

Later, the case went to court. After hearing the evidence, the judge ruled that the boy should stay in foster care. He thought that church three times a week was too much for anybody who didn't want to be there. The parents were not able to appeal the case to a higher court.

However, another case from Washington did make it to the Washington Supreme Court. It involved another girl in junior high. She was also informed by a visiting social worker that if she was having conflict with her parents, she could seek shelter in a foster home.

The "conflict" in this case involved the girl's desire to use drugs and sleep with her boyfriend. Her "abusive" parents did not want her to do these things, and they grounded her in an attempt to get her behavior under control. She found an ally in her local social worker.

The parents fought back in court. The trial judge made a specific finding that the parents had reasonable rules of behavior and that they were using reasonable means of discipline to enforce those rules of behavior. Nonetheless, because the legislature had enacted a law that deemed that conflict between a parent and child was a sufficient cause to remove the child from the home, the judge held that he was forced to continue to put the child in foster care.

The parents appealed to the Washington Supreme Court, arguing that this law was a violation of their constitutional rights as parents to direct the upbringing of their children. The court ruled against them, even though they agreed that the parents' rules and methods of discipline were both reasonable.

These parents asked me to appeal their case to the United States Supreme Court. I would have done so, but they came to me on the last day that an appeal can be filed and there was no time to prepare the fifty-plus pages of printed material required for such an appeal.

In other cases: A family had their teenage daughter removed from their home because she wanted to attend the junior prom and the parents chose to uphold their church's prohibition against dancing; a father in Iowa lost custody of his children to the state because he wanted to wait six months to see if his children really did need a tonsillectomy before doing surgery.

Social workers spend so much time investigating cases that are clearly outside the realm of reason that they are too busy to investigate the true cases of abuse and neglect. And far too often, I am keenly aware of the anti-Christian zeal that motivates many of these investigations.

The Long Ordeal of Betty Batey

There is one profession that rivals the social service profession for its anti-Christian attitudes. That is the mental health profession. Psychiatrists, psychologists, and counselors have often proven themselves to be enemies of Christian values and even individual Christians.

I am not saying that all mental health professionals are anti-Christian. Obviously, Dr. James Dobson is a Christian and applies his Christianity in his professional life, as do thousands of other Christian psychologists and therapists. But the majority of mental health professionals that I have dealt with in a number of cases have been subtly anti-Christian. A few have been blatantly so.

The right of Christian parents to raise their children in ways that please God are often threatened if the parents find themselves in a court proceeding that requires a psychological evaluation of their children. No case illustrates this problem better than the epic battle endured by Betty Batey in the courts of San Diego.

The object of this legal struggle was Betty's son Brian. Betty had married Frank Batey, who was a professing, church-going Christian. But the truth was that before, during, and after their marriage, he was a practicing homosexual. Their marriage finally ended in divorce and Betty was granted custody of Brian, who was then about six.

Things went along acceptably for a few years, but eventually Brian became aware of his father's open homosexuality and refused to go on his weekend visitations. His father slept with his homosexual partner, and many men swam nude in the pool at their southern California home. There was also strong evidence of drug use in the home.

Betty refused to force Brian to go on these visitations. But it was Brian's refusal to go that stopped the visits.

Betty was repeatedly hauled into court for contempt for her failure to send Brian on visitations. Eventually, the judge ordered a hearing on change of custody. The stars of this hearing were psychologists and counselors who testified on behalf of Frank Batey.

One of the psychologists, Wardell Pomeroy, is a noted specialist in "sexology" from San Francisco. He is a coauthor of the Kinsey report, and also testifies regularly on behalf of porn dealers in obscenity trials. He had interviewed Frank Batey and his homosexual partner, but never once interviewed Betty Batey. Based solely on the information that Frank was a homosexual, while Betty was a Pentecostal Christian, Pomeroy testified that Frank would be the better parent. His "professional opinion" was that a fundamental Christian parent will "warp" a child's sexual development, while a homosexual parent will give a child an open and proper opportunity for sexual development.

If you think this testimony is so silly it would be rejected automatically, you need to know the outcome of the case. Based on Pomeroy's opinion and other related testimony, Frank Batey was awarded custody of Brian!

Betty Batey didn't sit still. She was now in the position of getting Brian for weekend visits, and she decided to follow the example of Joseph and Mary who escaped with their baby to Egypt. Betty escaped to another part of the country so that she could protect Brian. She and Brian fled to Texas, where they lived for nearly two years.

Betty was informed that law enforcement officials were

on her trail, so she left for Denver. There a pastor encouraged her to turn herself in to the FBI. My first contact with Betty was in the Denver jail awaiting transfer back to San Diego.

We went through several different trials together—a criminal contempt of court hearing, and two stages of a criminal trial on charges of kidnapping. God granted us victories in all of these criminal charges. Ultimately a judge ruled that Betty did not have a criminal motive; rather, her desire was simply to protect her son. He dismissed the felony charges.

But the major trial was a nine-week retrial on the issue of the custody of Brian Batey. Betty asked that custody be returned to her. Frank sought to have Brian returned to his home in Palm Springs where he lived with his partner.

A number of witnesses in the trial were mental health professionals. We had an extraordinarily difficult time getting any help from Christians in this field, and the battle was not easy.

First of all, Wardell Pomeroy returned to testify from San Francisco. I went to his office to take his deposition. Given his national reputation I expected to see him in a first-class high rise office building overlooking the bay. Instead, his office was housed in a store-front operation in a somewhat seedy part of town. There were pornographic films for rent or sale in the outer waiting room. And in his personal office, all four walls were stacked with books and magazines from floor to ceiling. There were some scholarly books, but the majority were pornography.

I had an opportunity to grill Pomeroy in preparation for trial. One series of questions revealed the depth of his perverted thinking. I asked: "What would be your clinical objective if you had an adult male client who stated that he was having sex with a seventeen-year-old girl?"

"I would find out why he was concerned—what was making him feel guilty about this relationship, and help him relieve his guilt," Pomeroy replied.

"And what would be your objective if your client was having sex with a ten-year-old?" I asked.

He said that he saw where I was going with this, and refused to say that there was anything morally wrong with sexual activities no matter what the age of the child. To him, it would simply be a matter of dealing with the guilt.

He repeated his testimony from the first trial: All things being otherwise equal, he would always recommend a homosexual parent over a fundamentalist Christian parent. "The Christian will harm the child's sexual and emotional development," he repeated.

A local psychologist also testified that Frank Batey was the preferable parent. He performed a number of psychological tests on Frank and Betty. Based on his tests he concluded that Frank was more honest than Betty and accordingly preferred Frank as the parent. One of the tests was the draw-a-person test. Frank was quite a good artist and did very well. Betty can't draw a lick and did poorly. The psychologist put a great deal of emphasis on the fact that Betty's people had no feet, suggesting she had no roots or stability in her life. These tests "proved" Frank's honesty to this doctor's satisfaction.

On cross-examination I pointed out a number of lies that Frank Batey had told the psychologist. For example, he claimed to have sold an article to *Playboy* magazine as one of the sources of his income. In reality, he had written a letter-to-the-editor condemning Jerry Falwell, for which he obviously received no money.

Even when confronted with such lies, the psychologist clung to his conclusion about Frank's honesty as the "preferred" parent.

The lawyers for the homosexuals were also able to secure the assistance of a world-renowned child psychiatrist from Los Angeles. This man testified that Brian's moral development was "stunted" for his age of fourteen. I asked what he meant by that, and he explained that Brian believed things in "black and white." He said, for example, that most seven-year-olds say it's always wrong to steal, while most fourteen-year-olds say it's wrong to steal unless you need to steal bread to avoid hunger or for other "justifiable" reasons.

I asked him what about a thirty-four-year-old (my age at that time), who believes that it is always wrong to steal. He replied, "That's your fixation."

He blamed Betty for the fact that Brian's moral development was immature because she had taught him that it is always wrong to steal. And for this and other related reasons, he recommended that Frank be awarded custody.

At the end of the nine-week trial the judge put Brian in a Christian foster home and Christian school that we recommended as our alternative if the judge would not give Betty custody. But Brian ultimately ended up with his father. (This was not the end of the matter, though, and we will come back to the Bateys in Chapter 18.)

What are we to think of this? A profession that consistently says homosexuality is better than Christianity, that a parent who teaches moral absolutes is warping the child's development, and that decides real-life lies aren't relevant in determining honesty can be very dangerous to those of us trying to live by the Word of God. I would urge strong caution in dealing with any member of this profession. Even if the person is a professing Christian, check to see if his advice is rooted in God's Word rather than in theories of Freud, Jung, or Fromm. He might be willing to let "you be you" for your own life, but may be actively opposed to your "inflicting Christian principles upon an innocent child."

How Do You Draw the Line?

One area of parents' rights most likely to be challenged is the child-discipline practice of spanking. I would urge you to read Rick Fugate's excellent book *What the Bible Says About Child Rearing,* or *Dare to Discipline* by Dr. James Dobson. Follow their advice in employing moderate means of spanking.

First, it's important to discipline your child *in private.* This prevents your child from being embarrassed in front of others. From a legal perspective, it is a doubly good idea. You should never, never spank a child in public these days. A police car or social services worker may be sitting at your door when you get home if someone who disagrees with spanking witnesses such an occurrence.

Second, if you get a call from a social worker or a similar

government official who informs you that there has been a report about your family and an investigation is required, do not verbally agree to an investigation or give any information on the phone. The only thing you should say is that you are going to talk with your spouse and your lawyer, and that you will get back to them.

Although it may involve a little expense, I strongly urge you to at least consult initially with a lawyer. Do-it-yourself solutions may cost you the custody of your children. Find a lawyer who deals with these issues on a fairly regular basis and who is aggressive in protecting the rights of parents.

Third, children are repeatedly told that if their parents are abusing them, they should call the child-abuse hotline. This message is regularly communicated at school and on television. Obviously, you should not abuse your child and should seek help immediately if you are doing so. But there is a great deal of argument about what constitutes child abuse. If your child gets mad because of a reasonable form of discipline, there may be a temptation to call the child-abuse hotline to fight back against your parental authority.

It's a good idea to make sure that your children know the danger of calling such a hotline in a fit of anger. They can cause enormous disruption to their own lives by being placed in foster care for an extended period of time. It will also cost their family dearly in terms of unity, emotions, and finances.

I believe, however, that children need to have a godly alternative to the child-abuse hotline. Tell your children that if they believe there is a serious dispute between you and them and they feel a need for protection, they have your permission to call their grandparents, aunts or uncles, or your pastor. Choose someone who shares your basic values and also has the love and respect of your children. If you are mistreating your children, you need to be called to task. More than likely, the child's grandparent or pastor can help give them the necessary perspective to understand the discipline they are receiving.

Fourth, work for a long-range solution to solve the excesses of the child-abuse industry. Groups like Family Research Council and Concerned Women for America regularly work for laws that try to regain the legal rights of parents that we traditionally enjoyed. A group that specializes in this topic is VOCAL (Victims of Child Abuse Laws). Although it is not specifically a Christian organization, it shares the traditional values of proper parental rights to discipline and moral upbringing of children.

Fifth, work for legislative solutions to restore the right of parents to be the primary adults allowed to make judgments for their children. Your county government has the ability to restrict those librarians who desire to give your children R-rated materials. Your state government has the ability to pass laws restoring parental rights in the areas of birth control and abortion. You should contact your local officials in both spheres to make sure that they are voting to restore your rights as parents in these and related efforts.

———

Joanne should tell Sarah Jones from the Department of Children's Services that she is very sorry, but she will not be able to come out right away. She should inform the social worker that she will need to contact a lawyer, and that either she or the lawyer will get back to her promptly.

If Joanne cannot possibly obtain a lawyer, she should at least get a witness. Neither she nor her husband should talk with the official alone. Her pastor or some other adult should go with her.

She should not let the Children's Services worker be alone with her children or subject them to any kind of examination. If they claim they need to find out her child's physical condition, she should offer to take the child to the family doctor and have him write a letter to Children's Services stating his findings.

If a police officer appears at her house with a warrant, she must obey his directives. Even then, Joanne should ask him if she can call a lawyer immediately before he does anything with her children. No parent is ever required to answer the questions of a government official, including a police officer's. Tell them that you will be glad to answer any question that your lawyer tells you is appropriate.

The Rights of Christians on the Job

Jerry Wilson is employed as a computer operator by a large private company. On his lunch hour he routinely sits at his desk, eats his lunch, and reads his Bible. He sometimes uses the time to prepare the Sunday school lesson he teaches to high school students.

Recently, he talked with fellow employees about having a once-a-week lunchtime Bible study. The meetings began, held in a corner of the office cafeteria. People seated nearby could hear what was going on, but the conversation was no louder than other groups gathered at lunch and discussing sports, politics, or other random items of conversation.

Jerry got a call from management. He was told that he was improperly injecting religion into a secular work environment, and was directed to stop the Bible study. And he could no longer read his Bible at his desk.

Jerry is forty-five years old. Employment in his industry has become stagnant. It's a difficult time in his life to be thinking about switching jobs. He fears that if he bucks management on this one, he may be on his way out. His kids are getting near college age. There is so much at risk. Yet, Jerry genuinely wants to stand up for his beliefs. What should he do?

Discrimination against Christians in the workplace is gaining momentum. Christians working for government institutions have long taken the brunt of such discrimination, which has seemed acceptable and even "mandated" because of misguided notions about separation of church and state.

Discrimination Against Christians in Government Service

Witnessing in the military prompts court-martial

One of the first religious freedom cases I handled was on behalf of an enlisted man in the Navy, named Jack Gaddis. Jack was facing court-martial charges for going door-to-door in officer's housing, inviting people to come to his church and witnessing to anyone interested.

There was a base policy that prohibited any door-to-door solicitation in base housing. However, the policy was not enforced when the Camp Fire Girls sold mints and cookies door-to-door. United Way workers were also allowed to solicit in the area, and newspaper vendors were permitted free access. A number of other exceptions to the rule were tolerated.

I tried to talk to the military commanders and the base lawyers, to no avail. So I wrote a brief in preparation for the trial and submitted it a few days in advance, pointing out that the Supreme Court held that military housing in the United States was not exempt from the rules of First Amendment law applicable to civilian housing. It was also a denial of "equal protection" to allow so many other kinds of door-to-door activity while they singled-out religious activity for punishment. The day before trial, the military lawyer called me and said that his superiors had directed him to drop all charges.

Witnessing done on one's own time cannot be used as a basis for disciplinary action, even if it is on government property—so long as other kinds of free speech activities are not banned for other employees in this locale.

Christian service in the community leads to disciplinary action against teacher

Marie Russo is one of the gutsiest young women I have ever met. She was employed as a first-year science teacher at a public high school in northern New Jersey. She "got in trouble" when she organized an alternative-to-Halloween party, held in the evening off campus. Marie said nothing to students about the party during the school day, or while on school property. Students in her church passed the word to other students. Marie paid for the entire party, including the cost of hiring a contemporary Christian band to attract the students. Toward the end of the party, Marie presented the gospel to the entire group of students who had come voluntarily.

One student of a different religious faith told his mother about the party, and this woman complained to the principal. He and the superintendent took action, placing Marie under discipline. They told her that they would not permit her to do anything else of this nature, and she was specifically directed to stop going door-to-door in her church's witnessing program. These men stated that students might be "unduly influenced" if a teacher showed up at their door witnessing for Jesus.

It's interesting that teachers union groups are actively involved in political campaigns. They go door-to-door all the time, urging people to vote for a particular political candidate. You can be guaranteed that if one of their members was told to stop this door-to-door political activity because it might "unduly influence" students and their families, the union would have flown to the teacher's defense. Because of New Jersey law and the local teachers union contract, Marie was required to be a member of the union—but the union did absolutely *nothing* to help a Christian teacher facing discrimination because of activity that was clearly outside the scope of her employment.

Marie was not only disciplined, but also her job contract for the next year was not renewed because of these issues.

At the time, I was general counsel for Concerned Women for America. On Marie's behalf, I filed a federal civil rights lawsuit against the school district. After some face-to-face meetings with school officials and their lawyer, they conceded that they'd made the wrong decisions about Marie. They reversed all of their negative rulings, and simply asked that Marie continue her practice of not initiating religious discussions during class time. They agreed that she was permitted to briefly answer students' questions if they asked her about her own views. (One student later asked her what a person had to do to become a Christian. Another asked her to explain the Second Coming.)

Actions taken by a Christian off-the-job site and after-job hours cannot be the subject of disciplinary action, even though these after-hours activities might involve interaction with those who identify you as a government employee.

Teacher faces discipline for reading his Bible

Concerned Women for America has represented a Christian teacher from Denver in a case before the United States Supreme Court. Ken Roberts was charged with the "offense" of keeping his Bible on his desk and having three books about Christianity (among 200) in his classroom library. Ken also read silently from his Bible on occasion when the students were assigned a period of independent reading. There was no question of facing disciplinary action if he chose to read communist literature or a New Age book on transcendental meditation.

Prior cases have ruled against any kind of teacher-led Bible study on a public-school campus. But there is real hope that the Supreme Court is going to reverse the decision against Ken. If so, Bible reading by a teacher in a school cannot be the basis for discriminatory action. Under current law, I would expect that any government worker or private employee, other than a public-school teacher, facing discipline for reading his Bible at his desk during free time could successfully win a religious discrimination lawsuit.

Federal warden removed from position for refusal to permit abortions for women prisoners

It is not simply outward expressions of religious faith that get Christian employees in trouble. I once provided some counsel to a federal prison official who was disciplined and transferred across the country *for refusing to sign the orders to permit the women prisoners to go to hospitals to get abortions*! He was second in command of a federal women's prison, and the guards were apparently having sex with the prisoners. The policy was to quietly send the women off for abortions, presumably at taxpayers' expense, but an order had to be signed. The assistant warden, who was a Christian, refused to play any role in the securing of an abortion.

His courageous stand resulted in a federal law protecting the rights of others in future similar circumstances. There are a number of "conscience laws" now on the books protecting the rights of Christian employees who refuse to participate in abortions on religious grounds. There is still room for improvement in the law, however, especially in light of the diminishment of the general principle of religious freedom by the Supreme Court. (See Chapter 11.)

Discrimination Against Christian Employees in the Private Sector

Christian journalist fired for creationist views

Forest Mims III, of Sequin, Texas, was recently canceled as a columnist by the magazine *Scientific American*. Since 1989, Mims wrote a regular column called the "Amateur Scientist." Mims was canceled for the sole reason that he is a creationist. This was discovered when the editor at *Scientific American* found that Mims had written articles for Christian magazines. Mims' "Amateur Scientist" columns had nothing to do with the issues of creation and evolution, but the magazine determined that they did not want to give anyone the impression that they were approving creationism.

Christian psychiatrists attacked for injecting religion into their practice

Two Christian psychiatrists have separately found themselves in trouble for "injecting" religion into their practice. The firing of a woman psychiatrist in Alexandria, Virginia, was recently upheld by a federal court. The primary charges against her were that she "improperly" injected her Christian faith into her practice and that she carried on both a religious and professional relationship with a few patients.

Another psychiatrist was suspended from hospital privileges in Kentucky because he prayed with some of his patients. Dr. William Cato, a staff psychiatrist at Hardin Memorial Hospital, was charged with "inappropriate behavior" for praying with one female patient. He openly admitted to praying with others as well.

Dr. Cato started the psychiatric unit at the hospital twenty-two years earlier when he was an atheist. He had "the very best humanistic training," according to his own statement. When he was an atheist, Dr. Cato never had any trouble. But when he became a Christian in 1980 and started living for the Lord, his troubles began.

Other Christians in this field can expect similar trouble in the days ahead. The American Psychiatric Association has issued a policy severely limiting the role of religion in the practice of psychiatry.

Christian manager fired for refusing to attend New Age training seminar

Not only are we Christians facing discrimination for our stand *for* Jesus Christ, we are also facing on-the-job harassment for refusing to participate in the practice and training of other religions. The manager of a Chevrolet dealership on the West Coast was fired for refusing to attend a training seminar offered by the Pacific Institute. This "institute" is a group offering employment and management seminars that are clearly New Age in character. When the Christian manager refused to attend this New Age seminar, he was fired. He fought his case in court and recently won.

The position of the Equal Employment Opportunity Commission (EEOC) is that compelled attendance at New Age seminars is a violation of federal law banning religious discrimination in the workplace.

The Double Harassment of Christian Women

More than a decade ago, long before it became a fashionable topic of conversation, I represented two different Christian women who faced sexual harassment and attack on their jobs. The legal precedents are much stronger since that time.

And although this has been portrayed as a "liberal" issue in the media, Christians should concur with the position that sexual pressure and filthy comments have no place anywhere in our nation, including on the job.

Many Christian women face a kind of double harassment. I heard recently of a woman who was ridiculed for her refusal to put up with any form of sexual innuendo. Because everyone knew her feelings stemmed from the fact that she was a Christian, they attacked her with additional jokes and comments, calling her "Virgin Mary."

This kind of harassment is not only doubly objectionable, it is doubly illegal. It is a violation of the law prohibiting religious discrimination, as well as prohibiting sexual harassment. No woman should take this kind of comment without complaint. Women workers should report this behavior to their supervisor in accordance with company policy. If that fails, contact the EEOC and get yourself a lawyer. (See Appendix.)

Where Do You Draw the Line?

Although there is a great deal of difference between the cases described in this chapter and the kinds of problems a number of Christians become embroiled in on the job, some general advice will apply.

First, do not get yourself in trouble for witnessing, reading the Bible, or praying at a time you are supposed to be working. Your employer has a right to expect that you are working during the time he is paying you.

But there is sometimes a subtle difference between inappropriate and appropriate behavior. Police officers, for example, often work with a partner. There are many times during the day when two police partners are engaged in normal conversation about sports, their families, or other non-job-related topics. At a time when such conversation is permitted, conversation about Christianity is also permitted. The general rule of law is: *Conversation cannot be limited on the basis of its specific content.*

But a police officer who is supposed to be conducting a criminal investigation should not be reading an offender John

3:16 at the point in time he is supposed to be reading the suspect his "Miranda" rights. Employers have the right to insist that during working periods, non-work-related activity be curtailed.

Second, many situations of workplace discrimination against Christians will have to be faced alone. There are some occasions when a Christian worker can get other believers to join with him or her in making a stand. Whenever this is possible, it is a good idea. It may be difficult to find other Christians willing to risk their employment, but if one or more others will stand with you, there will be extra power both spiritually and temporally.

Third, job harassment is another circumstance in which you should consider legal assistance. Two things as worthwhile as your faith and your job are worth defending. Employment discrimination is a field of law that can be very lucrative for lawyers. You may be able to find a lawyer willing to work on such a case on a contingency fee basis. That means that the lawyer agrees to take the case on a percentage of the final recovery against the employer. If you do not win, you owe nothing. You will only have to pay out-of-pocket costs in the meantime. (More about this in Chapter 16.)

Fourth, religious discrimination in employment is a violation of federal law. If you feel that you have been subjected to such discrimination, you can contact the EEOC.

Fifth, you may want to take your case of religious discrimination to the media. First, be sure your situation has been checked out by a lawyer or someone experienced in such matters. Religious discrimination is illegal, and you can often find a powerful ally in the media. Other times, potential friends and allies you would not have found on your own will come to your assistance if they read about the case in the newspaper.

––––––––

Jerry Wilson has suffered from a case of clear religious discrimination in employment. Even though he works for a private company, he still has a legal right to demand the protection of his civil rights.

Keep in mind that it would be entirely different if Jerry

was studying his Bible at a time when he was supposed to be doing his job. But during the lunch hour, he is entirely free to study the Bible either alone or with other workers.

Jerry should first appeal to his employer privately. If this doesn't work, he should contact both a lawyer and the EEOC.

$\diamond$ **8** $\diamond$

The Battle for the Church

First Bible Church needed a church secretary, so the board of elders authorized the pastor to run an ad in the local newspaper. Suzy Lawrence applied for the job and appeared to be qualified. She was offered the job and was supposed to start the following Monday. However, on Friday the pastor received a call from a member of the congregation who heard that Suzy was hired. The member knew Suzy and told the pastor that Suzy had been living with her boyfriend for the last ten months. The pastor called Suzy to confirm this information. Suzy confirmed the story, although she also made it very plain that she thought that her private life was her own business.

The pastor consulted with the elders. The next day, he got a call from a well-known local lawyer, threatening to sue the church for violation of the state law prohibiting discrimination on the basis of marital status.

The pastor and elders met to decide what to do about Suzy. Should they reverse their decision and refuse to hire Suzy and face a lawsuit? Where would you draw the line?

There are a number of areas of church ministry that have become legal concerns for the first time. Churches are starting to become victims of increasingly hostile lawsuits that go far beyond the "I fell down and got hurt on the church steps" kind of suit.

New legal threats to churches go to the very heart of biblical ministry. Churches have been sued for discrimination in employment against homosexuals. Churches have been restricted in the use of their own facilities, not for health or safety reasons, but merely because the building was deemed to have artistic or historical significance.

As both a church elder and lawyer specializing in religious liberty cases, I am alarmed at the growing insensitivity to the rights of churches. Lawyers and judges, like the rest of society, have become increasingly secular in their orientation. They tend to look upon churches as "just another business."

Let's look at a number of these new legal threats to church ministries to see what you and your church can do to meet these threats.

Legal Attacks on Church Employment Practices

In 1991, the legislature in Hawaii passed a state gay rights law. The law specifically exempts churches from the coverage of this law, but only as pertaining to the hiring of ministerial staff. Other staff, such as secretaries, teachers, church organists and janitors, are *not* exempted from the law.

In the 1970s, an Orthodox Presbyterian Church in San Francisco successfully defended a gay rights lawsuit brought by the former church organist who was fired for practicing homosexuality. The judge ruled that it was a violation of the Free Exercise Clause of the First Amendment to apply this law to a church. Because the Hawaii law is more specific and, more importantly, because of a terrible decision by the United States Supreme Court (see Chapter 11), the outcome of this issue is now much more likely to be in favor of homosexuals.

This Supreme Court decision also affects the rights of churches that hire only men as pastors. Most conservative Protestant churches and the Roman Catholic Church follow this practice.

There are some things that a church can do to prepare for such a suit. But there are some issues that cannot be avoided altogether, and the Christian community is going to have to join together to change the law.

Steps of Action to Protect Your Church

Every church should develop a written employment policy. Specify the qualifications for each position. It is a big mistake if you fail to require spiritual qualifications for every position in your church. Ideally, you should limit all employees to church members. Alternatively, you can limit employment to those who would be eligible for church membership, but who attend a church of a similar faith elsewhere. Churches need to have a written justification for requiring spiritual qualifications for every position.

For example, all staff should be expected to join in staff prayer meetings. All staff should be expected to be able to assist in primary spiritual counseling—at least to the extent that if a person expresses a desire to become a Christian, every staff member should be able to share the plan of salvation. Put such a requirement in their job description. If you have such requirements for all staff members, your church will be in a much better position to defend a potential employment discrimination suit. You are entitled to have spiritually qualified people if you expect them to share a part of the spiritual load.

Your employment policy should make it clear that any person may be immediately terminated if they begin a pattern of living that evidences a rejection of the spiritual principles of the church. We expect integrity of the legal and medical community. If a lawyer acts in an unprofessional manner against the interests of his clients, he faces disbarment. In the same manner, churches must police their own. We should not permit immoral or unscrupulous individuals to remain on the staff of our churches.

Counseling Malpractice

Attorney Shelby Sharpe, from Fort Worth, Texas, attended a church malpractice seminar put on by the American Bar Association. Lawyers bent on finding new ways to sue for large sums of money can use the material put out at this ABA seminar to target local churches and denominations.

Sharpe calls the seminar the coming "nuclear attack" against churches.

Grace Community Church, pastored by John MacArthur, was the target of the most highly publicized clergy malpractice case to date. His church was sued when a young man, who was in an ongoing counseling relationship with the church, took his own life. The case took years to resolve and ended in the church's favor. Attorney Sam Ericcson devoted years of his life to this defense, and the costs were staggering—far beyond what most local churches would ever be able to sustain.

The malpractice crisis is largely fueled by greed, coupled with the false belief that someone else must be responsible for all difficulties in life. If a patient doesn't get well, he sues his doctor. If a doctor truly makes a negligent mistake, he should bear the brunt of his failure. Far too often, such suits are contrivances to seek financial reward, when the doctor has performed reasonably.

This greed mentality is about to invade the church. Some lawyers will bring these cases out of financial motives alone. Others will bring these cases out of pure hatred toward the church.

How to Protect Your Church

There are several things churches can do to protect themselves from such lawsuits. First, *obtain liability insurance that provides "clergy or counseling malpractice" coverage.*

Second, *develop a written form to be signed by every person coming to a church staff member for counseling.* It should be clearly stated that the church is not providing psychological or psychiatric counseling, rather that counseling is spiritual in nature. The statement should cite the verse that Christians should refrain from suing each other, and that all counseling is undertaken with the understanding that both sides agree to abide by that premise. (See 1 Corinthians 6:1-8).

Some larger churches have licensed professional counselors or even psychologists on staff. The counseling done by these professionals needs to be handled in accordance with the usual standards of the profession—especially if there is any kind of a fee charged for the counseling.

Finally, *church staff members should keep good notes of every counseling session.* Immediately after the session is over, a few notes of the key points should be recorded. Strict confidentiality of these notes must be maintained.

It is a regrettable side effect of these types of suits that some churches may become reluctant to engage in the kind of counseling that works best. Psychologists usually have the goal of teaching people to cope. Spiritual counseling usually has the goal of helping people truly change and overcome problems. Churches need to continue to do what is right, but do what they can to protect themselves, as well.

Government Restrictions on the Use of Church Property

Zoning laws. When zoning laws were first introduced, they made a lot of sense. Coal-burning factories shouldn't be located next to schools or housing areas. Commercial areas should be separated from industrial factories and farms. But as cities and suburbs develop, zoning laws are becoming more and more regulatory for purely financial rather than health and safety reasons.

One of the innocent victims of the second generation of zoning laws are churches. For instance, the Cornerstone Bible Church in Hastings, Minnesota, found it virtually impossible to secure a permanent location. A new church, it quickly outgrew a home and rental locations. Finally, they found an old theater in a downtown commercial zone, which the church wanted to purchase and renovate.

The city zoning code kept the church out. Application was made to the city government, asking for an exception to the zoning code—and this was denied. The church was forced to take the city to court. Initially the city won its case, but a federal appeals court recently sent the case back to the lower court for a new trial. (Incidentally, the church prevailed on free speech and freedom of assembly grounds—not free exercise of religion.)

The real-life effect of zoning codes in most areas of the country is an artificial inflation of the cost of land that is properly zoned as a church. In many places, there is no land at all that churches have the *right* to occupy. In such circumstances, churches must apply for a special exception. Most zoning codes I have examined allow virtually every other kind of structure as a matter of right in at least one zone. The fact that churches must obtain zoning by special exception in every case adds tens of thousands of dollars in legal and engineering fees to every church structure.

In Fairfax County, Virginia, churches have found it virtually impossible to build an auditorium that seats more than 1,000 people. There are several churches that would become very large and they own plenty of land—in one case over 40 acres. But the county employs its zoning code fiercely and limits any church from getting too large.

This limitation works a double hardship on Christians in the county. New churches face real estate prices that are commonly as high as $10-$20 per square foot for properly zoned property. This means that a single acre of ground costs at least $430,000. Older churches are prohibited from becoming too large by virtue of the zoning code. New churches are priced out of the market by the fact that strict zoning has driven suitable property prices through the ceiling. And this is coupled with the fact that the Fairfax school district accelerates the price of renting public-school buildings each year that a church rents—and there is a seven-year deadline to get out entirely.

Such zoning laws are not for the protection of the people. They are weapons being used to squeeze churches out of existence.

Landmark laws. Another weapon the government has found to hamper church growth is the use of landmark laws. It sounds so wonderful to have your church designated an "historic landmark." Churches would probably invite the mayor to a Sunday service and warmly thank him when the landmark designation is first awarded.

Then the church finds out that there is a catch. A landmarked building cannot be altered without the consent of the government. And landmark commissions are typically controlled by those committed to maintaining the status quo.

Two churches recently lost the right to control their own buildings because of landmark laws. The First Covenant Church in Seattle took its case to the U.S. Supreme Court, claiming that taking over control of the church building for purely artistic reasons violated the church's right to religious freedom. They lost.

An Episcopal church in Manhattan lost a similar case in a federal appeals court. The building in question was a seven-story church office located next door to a historic church building. Both the church and the office building were designated as landmarks. The church wanted to tear down the old office building and build a new one, which would allow expansion of church programs and also provide millions of dollars in revenue through commercial office rentals. Purely artistic concerns overcame the church's right to use its building in a way that would allow the expansion of church programs.

Taxation of churches. I see the day rapidly approaching when churches are going to become subject to taxation. The legal groundwork has already been laid by the U.S. Supreme Court. We simply await the time for politicians desperate enough for money that they are willing to brave the outcries from churches.

In 1981, when I was a lobbyist in Washington State, a bill came before the legislature that was called a "technical corrections" bill. It unanimously passed the House of Representatives without debate because it appeared to be nothing more than an attempt to fix a few discrepancies in the state tax laws.

A Christian attorney serving in the legislature started thumbing through the bill shortly after he'd joined all his colleagues in approving it. He saw the word "church" buried deep in the legislation and called me to analyze the bill. After a thorough review, I was able to determine that deep in the "technical language" were hidden provisions that would cause over 80 percent of the churches in the state to lose their tax-exempt status.

As soon as that discovery was made, a full-scale alert was issued to hundreds of churches across the state. The outcry was so loud and so vehement that the bill never even got a hearing in the state Senate, and died without further action.

A handful of bureaucrats came perilously close to beginning the process of taxing churches by a few hidden words in a long, complex piece of legislation.

How to Protect Your Church

Zoning laws, landmark laws, and laws that will tax churches are all the product of state and local government. The only good way to battle such laws is by *preventative medicine.* The only way the Washington tax-the-churches-law was defeated was by the combined efforts of two Christians, one serving in the legislature and one working as a lobbyist for Christian causes.

This is the same way you can provide the best legal atmosphere in your state and community. Encourage some of the men in your church to dedicate a portion of their time to serving in state and local government. Some churches I know wisely encourage some of their men to perform this kind of community service. These churches have the wisdom to relieve such men from other significant church responsibilities so they can properly balance a job and family as well. Godly men who are willing to serve in this capacity have the opportunity to do a lot of good, not just for their own church but for all churches in their community.

The first mistake First Bible Church made was to advertise a church position in a newspaper. Anti-discrimination laws that may not otherwise be applicable can be triggered if a job is advertised in the paper.

Second, the church failed to establish spiritual standards for the job. A church secretary is a key player in the ministry of a church, and needs to have spiritual qualifications in a written job description.

Despite these errors, the church should stick to the right course of action and refuse to hire Suzy if she is living with a man outside of wedlock. I believe that one of a number of Christian legal organizations would welcome the opportunity to defend a church for free in such a scenario.

◇ **9** ◇

Keeping a "Right Spirit"

My natural tendencies caused one of my friends, who saw me in the midst of a political dispute, to say I sometimes react like a "trained doberman pincer." Other friends disputed this point: They thought it was more accurate to say "untrained." That's to say I did not always respond calmly or treat my opponents with dignity and respect. Sometimes I'd resort to the "character comments" that typify most political campaigns.

In the early 1980s, I was on a TV show in Seattle, with several dozen people in the audience. I was undergoing a lot of attack, and I didn't handle it particularly well because I felt it was important to defend myself. After the show, I responded in anger to one man who'd really come after me. I interrupted a conversation he was having. It turned out the man he was talking to was a Christian, who was calmly trying to deal with him. I butted in and ruined everything.

My wife, Vickie, had watched the show at home, and later told me I'd do a lot better if I'd respond more calmly and with a gentle spirit. She used an analogy that—afterward—spoke to me: "Getting your message across is a lot like singing a song. You have to do more than sing the right words. You need a pleasing melody if you want people to listen."

Soon I had an opportunity to put this lesson to the test. The American Library Association asked me to give a keynote address at their annual convention. They selected me because I was engaged in an ongoing dispute with a library over the showing of a sexually explicit movie to high school students.

Of all the groups and organizations I've ever been involved with, the American Library Association is by far the most liberal. In preparation for the speech, I reviewed their manuals, which teach librarians how to respond to people who criticize their actions. They give sample press statements and tell librarians to call people like me "censors" and other negative comments.

In my typical manner, I wrote a speech in which I told the American Library Association a thing or two. I really let them have it with both barrels blazing.

Fortunately, I practiced the speech before my toughest audience—Vickie. She said very little. Something like, "Well, hmmm." I knew what she was thinking. Right song, but that melody. . . .

I rewrote the speech.

In my new speech I did not tell the librarians how *wrong* they were for intentionally violating the rights of parents. I told them how parents *felt* about a situation where their child was given a sexually explicit book without their knowledge or consent. Instead of telling librarians that it was demagoguery to call people "censors," I appealed to them: Couldn't they see the difference between people who want to burn books, and people who merely want to exercise personal judgment on what their own children read and see?

When I finished, I got a surprising amount of applause. Then I sat down next to the man who was to follow me. He was a college professor, who was an expert on "censorship." He'd written a speech designed to attack me for being a hotheaded bigot and a right-wing idiot, and would have been a perfect response to the speech I'd torn up. I'd been set up for a roasting of the first degree, but thanks to Vickie's wisdom I escaped the flames.

The reaction later was truly gratifying. Dozens of librarians came up to me and said, "We're on your side! We know we are a minority, and we were so worried that our cause would suffer today. But it was *wonderful*. Keep up the good work."

The Library Association liked the speech so much they published it in their journal. The American Bar Association picked it up and published it as a feature article in their national magazine for young lawyers. As a result of that speech, I received a number of additional speaking engagements.

I believe the Lord poured out His blessing on me to demonstrate how important it is to have the right spirit in every circumstance—even when we're the intended object of ridicule before an audience of over 3,000 people.

This lesson is also important to remember when you think people *are not* watching you.

Some time ago, I was scheduled to speak in one church on Sunday morning and another church 250 miles away on Sunday night. I needed to catch a plane in order to keep this schedule. About 2 P.M. the airline called me to say that the flight was running very late and I was probably going to miss the second speaking engagement. Rather than my more natural response of anger, I answered very calmly and worked for a long time on the phone with the agent who'd called to find a substitute flight.

A couple days later, I got a letter from this same airline agent. At the very moment he was told that he needed to call me, he'd been reading an article about me in the Seattle *Times*. His letter told me that he was really wondering what kind of person I was, and whether or not the Christian principles I espoused were real. He said that my calm response to the cancellation was unexpected, and it confirmed for him that my cause of fighting for moral laws must be just because of the spirit he sensed in me during our call. He also enclosed a very generous check to support my organization.

I was humbled and driven to my knees in gratitude to God. Better than anyone else, I knew that my response to him wasn't the natural "Mike Farris." It was the Spirit-controlled version that had won the day.

I've had many chances to see other Christians in situations where they've had to draw the line against secular opposition. It's sad to say, but far too often we Christians can respond rudely with arrogance or harshness. I've already mentioned the man who hinted that God would kill members of a legislative committee if they voted the wrong way.

In the famous "Nebraska 7" case, certain of the people involved responded with a very harsh spirit. Others, like Pastor Bob McCurry, stood strong and without compromise—but there was such a sweet spirit about the man that he stood out as a good witness for our Lord.

Let me share four things that can help you overcome the temptation to respond with anger or harshness:

When You're Tempted to Anger

Do not defend yourself. In Luke 5:39, Jesus instructs us to turn the other cheek when we're attacked. In Luke 12:11, He tells us not to worry about what we're going to say when we are attacked for His sake. This is a very difficult thing to do. But remember we are not called to be witnesses for our self; we are witnesses for our Lord. You are there to defend *God's* principles, not your own reputation. And let me assure you, your reputation will be enhanced tremendously if you respond calmly. Proverbs 3:3–4 says: "Let love and faithfulness never leave you; bind them around your neck, write them on the tablet of your heart. Then you will win favor and a good name in the sight of God and man."

People will assume that you are being unjustly accused if your spirit serves as an unspoken answer to personal attacks and criticism. Remember, God *will* defend His people when they are oppressed. (See Jeremiah 50:33–34.)

Do not associate with hotheads. "Do not make friends with a hot-tempered man, do not associate with one easily angered, or you may learn his ways and get yourself ensnared" (Proverbs 22:24–25). If a group of parents is going to speak to the school board about an issue, do everything you can to prevent a known hothead from getting to the microphone. If one hothead joins your group, it will taint the reputation of all. Find a constructive job for this person—behind the scenes.

Remember that there are more battles ahead. When I was on the TV show in Seattle, part of the reason I was so upset is that I was not given a chance to fully state my position on some important issues. I finally learned that life is more than one 60-minute TV show. And the reputation I make will last a lot longer than the specific points I say on any particular broadcast.

Be patient. Don't get angry if you get cut off or lose a particular round. "A patient man has great understanding, but a quick-tempered man displays folly" (Proverbs 14:29). "Better a patient man than a warrior, a man who controls his temper than one who takes a city" (Proverbs 16:32).

Another side of this same point is that we cannot become complacent if we do well a few times. Even though I learned the importance of keeping the right spirit more than a decade ago, from time to time I still blow it. *Every* battle must be faced with a strong but calm and gentle spirit.

Keep in mind that there are more important issues at stake than the particular topic being debated. Let me illustrate this point with a story.

Once I received an invitation to return to the college I attended as an undergraduate to debate Timothy Leary, the LSD guru of the late 1960s. Our topic was "The Moral Majority." The debate was held in a sold-out auditorium in front of about 3,000 students and citizens from the community. It was also being recorded for television broadcast in three major cities.

I thought I did pretty well and kept the right spirit the whole time. In fact, when the debate came to a close, Timothy Leary told me that if he ever got busted again he might call me to be his lawyer.

I went home thinking I'd done a good job of presenting the importance of standing for the right principles in government and public life. I'd gotten the right message to over 3,000 people live, and to thousands more by television.

It wasn't until a year later that I learned the most important thing that was accomplished that night. The student body president who had set up the debate called me again. He asked me to speak alone to a student audience on the subject of abortion. I accepted, especially since it was an opportunity for Vickie and me to return to the college where we met.

In the dressing room before the speech, the student body

president came in to talk with me. He confessed that the year before he'd chosen both Leary and me because he thought that we were both "jokes" and would provide marvelous entertainment for the audience. Leary had dealt very harshly with them, demanding big money for the event. On the other hand, I'd been content to receive gas money and a hotel room. He said that he watched me a lot during the day's events and, of course, during the debate. He said he was really surprised in what he saw in my life, and as a result he began to attend a Baptist church near campus to investigate Christianity. He told me that six months later he received Jesus Christ as his Savior. He was even planning to attend seminary the next year.

This is the only time in my life I know of that any person has gotten saved simply as a result of observing my life. Nothing else I did at that debate could compare with the fact that one soul came to know Christ as a result of seeing a Christian exhibit a spirit of gentleness and self-control. "Though I am free and belong to no man, I make myself a slave to everyone, to win as many as possible" (1 Corinthians 9:19).

Remember, sometimes the *way* you draw a line may be the line between heaven and hell for a person who is watching.

Thus far, we've been discussing responses of a more personal nature—defending *your* children, *your* job, and *your* rights as parents. It is extremely important that we defend these areas of responsibility with an exemplary attitude. The next section in the book is going to deal with issues of a broader scope.

There are those Christians who look at a problem in their community and feel a need to pray for a solution. They should remember to pray in earnest. There are others who will see the same problem and say, "Someone should do something about this." Such people can provide moral and financial support for a third kind of person. These are Christians who look at a problem, like a new porno theater, and say, "Not in my community they won't!" These are the people called to frontline battles.

No matter which level of involvement is consistent with your personal calling and gifting, you should remember two things. First, you need to have an appreciation for each kind of Christian—those who pray, those who support, and those who lead. Second, all of us need to remember that when we fight, our spirit will have a far greater effect than our actions.

Let's take a look at how some broader battles are going and what you might do to help.

The Battle for Religious Freedom

Most Christians I've encountered are unaware of the most devastating Supreme Court decision since *Roe* v. *Wade*. On April 17, 1990, the Court issued an opinion in *Employment Division* v. *Smith,* and it is no exaggeration to say its decision in this case is as bad for religious freedom as *Roe* v. *Wade* was for the unborn. Our most precious liberty—the free exercise of religion—has been thrown into the constitutional garbage can.

Simply, out of the blue, five justices on the Court decided that religious freedom was a "luxury" our nation could no longer afford. The majority said while religious belief is protected, religious conduct is subject to government regulation.

Justice Sandra Day O'Connor, writing in dissent, demonstrated the fundamental error of the other justices' opinions:

> Because the First Amendment does distinguish between religious belief and religious conduct, conduct motivated by sincere religious belief, like the belief itself, must therefore be at least presumptively protected by the Free Exercise Clause. The Court today, however, interprets the Clause to permit the government, without justification, conduct mandated by an individual's religious belief, so long as that prohibition is generally applicable. But a law that prohibits certain conduct—conduct that happens to be an act of worship for someone—manifestly does prohibit that person's free exercise of his religion.

You may be asking, how could such a decision be made? Why haven't I heard about it? Let me take you inside the world of First Amendment constitutional law to strip away some of the outer layers of this decision so that you can clearly understand how badly we have been damaged by this decision.

How a "Sneak Attack" Took Place

Every important case decided by the Supreme Court has two parts: (1) the holding and (2) the supporting principles of law. The *holding* is the part of the case that says one person wins and the other person loses. For example, in *Roe* v. *Wade,* Roe was the unmarried woman seeking the right to an abortion; Wade was the district attorney in Dallas, Texas. Roe won the case, Wade lost. But by the time the case reached the Supreme Court, Roe had already had her baby. The bottom line of the case wasn't really that important on a personal level to either Roe or Wade.

It was the second part of the decision—*the supporting principles of law*—that became important to all of us. The reasoning given by the Court to support its decision creates what lawyers usually call the *precedent. Roe* v. *Wade* established the precedent that all state laws restricting abortion were unconstitutional. These supporting principles of constitutional law are far more important than the underlying facts of the case or the holding concerning the two parties.

In *Employment Division* v. *Smith* (we'll just call it *Smith* for reference), neither the facts of the case nor the holding are really that important. Let's look at them briefly, though, so we can set the case in context.

Two Native American Indians were employed as drug counselors in Oregon. They were members of the Native American Church and as a part of a church ritual took the drug peyote. Their employer found out about the drug use and concluded that drug counselors shouldn't be taking drugs for any reasons, including religious reasons, and fired them. Taking peyote for any reason is illegal under Oregon law.

They applied for unemployment compensation, but were denied because it was held that they were fired for good cause. They argued that since their firing was based on their religious practices, it was a denial of their right to the free exercise of religion to deny their claim for unemployment compensation.

In the Supreme Court, the case boiled down to one issue: Does the Free Exercise Clause of the First Amendment protect the right of Native Americans to take peyote for religious reasons?

Few constitutional experts expected the Native Americans to win their case. Under traditional rules of religious freedom, it was predictable that the Court would rule that even though religious freedom is a fundamental right of the highest order, it is not an absolute right. Given the severe nature of the drug problems in this country, it is appropriate for the government to ban all drug use, even drug use for religious purposes. In fact, this is essentially what Justice Sandra Day O'Connor wrote in her opinion. She voted against the Indians in the *holding*, but voted for a high view of religious freedom in her discussion of *constitutional principles.*

The five-justice majority saw things quite differently. They too voted against the Native Americans, as expected. But the principles of constitutional law they announced were both astonishing and devastating.

Two Levels of Constitutional Rights

What does this mean for the average person—for you and me?

The majority ruled that the Free Exercise of Religion will no longer be treated as a fundamental constitutional right. The Court has established two levels of constitutional rights—fundamental rights and ordinary rights. *Fundamental rights* include freedom of speech, freedom of the press, and freedom of assembly. *Ordinary rights* are general rights of equal protection and due process. For example, a person has the right to grow his hair as long as he wants, but if he is in public school or the military his right to long hair is not given nearly as much constitutional consideration as the right to freedom of speech or freedom of the press.

It is very important to know whether or not the courts will treat a certain right as a fundamental right or an ordinary right. If a fundamental right is at issue—the government has the burden of proof and must show an overwhelmingly important reason before they can deny a person's fundamental right. If an ordinary right is at issue—the individual has the burden of proof and as long as the government is acting reasonably, the government can override a person's ordinary constitutional right. Simply put, the government usually loses fundamental rights cases and usually wins cases based on ordinary rights.

The Court said treating the free exercise of religion as a fundamental right was a "luxury" our nation can no longer afford. The principle of law it announced was this: No constitutional religious exceptions will be granted for laws of general application.

This is where the rubber meets the road. There are laws of general application that prohibit discrimination against women in employment. Many conservative Protestant churches and the Roman Catholic Church hire only men as pastors. Before *Smith*, a church would have had a clear constitutional protection for their right to hire only men. That protection was removed by *Smith*.

Churches can now be sued by homosexuals for refusing to hire them if there is a city or state gay rights law. Before *Smith*, the Free Exercise Clause would bar such a suit. Now there is no such protection.

Were Conservative Christians Deceived?

You may be thinking, "The liberals got us again. First it was *Roe* v. *Wade* and abortion. Now it's this *Smith* decision and our religious freedom." I've got news for you. It wasn't the liberals on the Court who did this to us. It was the conservatives whom we cheered when they were appointed to office.

The majority decision was written by Justice Anthony

Scalia, a noted conservative who was appointed by President Reagan. In other areas of law, Justice Scalia is simply an excellent judge. He was joined by Chief Justice Rehnquist, and Justices White, Kennedy, and Stevens. Stevens is a liberal. The rest are all conservatives.

As we noted earlier, Justice Sandra Day O'Connor agreed with the majority on the holding (i.e. the Indians lose) but strongly disagreed with the decision to throw the free exercise of religion off the list of fundamental constitutional rights. I fully agree with her entire opinion. The three liberals on the Court, Marshall, Brennan, and Blackmun, agreed with her discussion of the law, but voted in favor of the Native American Indians.

Why are these conservatives opposed to a high view of the free exercise of religion? We can get some insight into such conservative thinking by looking at a column that George Will wrote concerning the *Smith* decision. On the Sunday after the Court issued the decision, Will wrote a syndicated column praising the opinion. He urged the Court to go even further and reverse *Wisconsin* v. *Yoder,* the decision that protects the right of parents to direct the education of their children in a manner consistent with their religious beliefs. Will declared:

> A central purpose of America's political arrangements is the subordination of religion to the political order, meaning the primacy of democracy. The Founders, like Locke before them, wished to tame and domesticate religious passions of the sort that convulsed Europe. They aimed to do so not by establishing religion but by establishing a commercial republic—capitalism. They aimed to submerge people's turbulent energies in self-interested pursuit of material comforts.

Will distorts history and defames our founding fathers. In signing the Declaration of Independence the founders voluntarily pledged their "lives, fortunes, and sacred honor" to establish a nation committed to principles of freedom. They certainly believed in free enterprise. But they would not have sacrificed their economic well-being if they were merely trying to establish a capitalist empire. Allegiance to capitalism was perfectly consistent with continuing rule by Great Britain. It was for freedom—religious freedom, political freedom, and personal freedom—that the founders put their fortunes on the line.

Will's views, though historically distorted, give us an important insight into the views of an important branch of the conservative movement. This is the branch for whom money is god—at least in terms of their operational political philosophy. They believe that allowing religious views to prevail is economically disruptive and "not cost effective." That view is expressed by the declaration of the Supreme Court that religious freedom is a "luxury" our nation can no longer afford. These conservatives have confused a luxury with a priceless treasure.

In my opinion, Christian conservatives have been used and manipulated by this other brand of conservatives who wanted our help to put their kind of people into important offices. We may yet learn from hard lessons like these: *We need to demand more from our political leaders as a condition of our support.* At a minimum we need to make sure that judges we are asked to support have an abiding respect for our history of religious liberty. Those who share the "conservative" view that our religious "passions" should be subsumed into self-interested economic pursuits do not deserve our support.

Surprising as it appears, it seems the Supreme Court carefully selected a case involving a very unpopular religious practice in order to change the law of religious freedom.

Just a few days before the decision, I had a case before the Supreme Court involving a Christian school in Massachusetts. The Court refused to hear it. I also asked the Supreme Court to take the *Mozert* case, involving the religious freedom of students and parents in the public school; the Court refused. For two or three years before issuing the *Smith* opinion, the Court carefully ducked case after case involving religious practices that are shared by a good portion of the American public. In my opinion, the Court wanted to pick a case that factually would not upset the American public. If they had denied religious freedom in the context of the *Mozert* case, Christians would have marched in the streets in protest. The Court is undoubtedly sensitive about the March for Life and I believe they hoped to avoid a similar episode.

Cases Decided After *Smith* Demonstrate Its Devastating Effect

A review of the cases that have followed the *Smith* decision make it clear that this decision means that everyone's religious freedom will be denied—not just Native Americans who take drugs. Since the Court announced its decision, every single free exercise of religion case that has been decided by the lower federal courts has been decided *against* the church or religious individual seeking constitutional protection.

Amish, Baptists, Catholics, Muslims, and the Salvation Army have all lost religious freedom claims in federal court. Churches in Seattle and New York City have lost the right to control their own buildings. Under the old rules of religious freedom, as long as a church complied with safety codes, government could not exercise control over church buildings. These two cases granted government control over churches simply because the governments wanted to preserve the artistic nature of church architecture. In the New York City case, it was agreed that the decision would cost the church millions of dollars and significantly hamper expansion of church ministries.

Roman Catholic prisoners lost a case concerning their right to have rosaries in their cells. Jewish prisoners lost a case where they asked the court to allow them to wear *yarmulkes*, the head covering worn by Orthodox Jews. The court told them to wear baseball caps like the other prisoners.

Some of the lower federal courts expressed genuine dismay that the *Smith* case forced them to deny claims of religious freedom. Others seemed content to deny both churches and religious individuals the free exercise of their faith.

Some of these cases would have been unsuccessful under the traditional rules of religious freedom. But many of the claims of churches and religious individuals would have been protected against government intrusion. Any rule of constitutional law that results in the 100 percent denial of religious liberty is not acceptable in America.

Fighting to Reverse This Decision

Fortunately, there are a group of Americans committed to overturning the effects of the *Smith* decision. A bill entitled the Religious Freedom Restoration Act (RFRA) was pending before Congress in early 1992. A group of lawyers representing a wide variety of religious and political views got together to draft this law, and I was made chairman of this drafting committee. The coalition supporting this legislation is an unexpectedly broad group and some of the organizations supporting this bill will astonish Christians nationwide.

The ACLU and the National Association of Evangelicals support this legislation. Concerned Women for America and People for the American Way went head-to-head in the *Mozert* case, yet they both support the RFRA. The Christian Life Commission of the Southern Baptist Church (the conservative group) and the Baptist Joint Committee (the liberal group) both are supporting organizations.

Most Christians believe that the ACLU and similar organizations hate Christianity. They have certainly earned this reputation by doing everything they can to drive Christianity out of the public schools and other public institutions. Make no mistake about it, the ACLU is wrong at least 90 percent of the time. But once in a while they take a correct position. The ACLU has consistently taken a good position in favor of home schooling, for example. In a case I handled in Michigan, we represented two home-schooling families—one Christian and one secular. The ACLU filed a friend-of-the court brief on behalf of only one family—the Christian family. They argued that Michigan law violated their religious freedom. The ACLU also came to the defense of the Moral Majority of Washington when a state agency tried to stop the circulation of a magazine exposing candidates' views on moral issues. The way to understand the ACLU is this: They will always support a broad view of the constitutional right in question, and will always oppose the government's views in such cases.

Who's Who

I have a system for analyzing all lobbying groups in Washington, D.C., that helps explain these coalitions. Each group can be categorized—at least in part—by their operational view of God. Some groups believe that man is god. The ACLU generally fits this category. Others believe that the state is god. Folks like Ted Kennedy fit this category, since he appears to believe that every problem of man can be solved by the government. The third group, represented by George Will, believes that money is god. And finally, there are those of us who believe that God is God. By supporting the RFRA, the man-is-god, state-is-god, and God-is-God groups have all joined together to advance religious freedom against the attack of the money-is-god crowd.

The way the coalition reached an agreement was to write the bill to endorse the general principle that the free exercise of religion is a fundamental freedom, without taking a position on any particular case. Like the Gulf War, there are certain things that draw Americans of virtually all political stripes together to work for the good of the country. This is one of those rare occasions.

The RFRA has a good chance of passage, but it may take a few years to get all the way through Congress. (You can call your congressmen, or write to my office to get an update. See the Appendix for my address.)

Your Part

There are three things you can do to advance the battle for religious freedom in this country:

1. Check the status of the RFRA. Until it is signed into law, it is entirely appropriate to urge your congressmen and senators to support this important legislation.

2. Do not let local and federal politicians gain your sup-

port without stating their position on religious freedom. And don't let them talk in generalities; make sure they are willing to vote to reverse the *Smith* decision. Also make sure they will support judicial candidates who endorse the principles of treating religious liberty as a fundamental freedom.

3. Support the organizations that fight for religious freedom. Groups like Christian Advocates Serving Evangelism and Concerned Women for America deserve your support for their consistent and cooperative efforts for religious freedom. (Other fine groups are listed in the Appendix.)

◊ 11 ◊

The Battle for Moral Sanity

America is reaping the harvest of a generation raised without a moral foundation. Babyboomers exploded the moral guidelines of their parents. And though it seems impossible, the children of boomers are even further down the moral spiral from their parents. Although there are many manifestations of our national moral failure, five problems persistently cause the greatest concern: abortion, drug and alcohol abuse, pornography, homosexuality, and divorce.

There are organizations that have specialized in seeking a solution to each of these problems on a national level. There is so much material available on these topics and so much work to be done, it would take an entire book to give a full treatment of each issue. Rather than trying to analyze national solutions to these problems, let's consider some steps of local action that you can take to improve the moral climate of your local community.

Battles on the Home Front

Abortion

Statistics for the latest year available (1989) indicate that 1.4 million unborn children were killed last year in this country. It is staggering to imagine that in forty years, the span of one generation, we will kill 56 million Americans. Here are a few steps of action we can take to save some of those lives.

Establish a goal of making your city or county an abortion-free zone. In many counties there are only one or two abortion providers. You may be able to exert pressure that is legally unassailable, and cause that number to be reduced to zero.

Take whatever steps you can to get all local hospitals to prevent the practice of abortion. If the hospital is government operated, you need to place influence on those elected officials who have responsibility for hospital policy. It is possible that you can convince Christians to fill enough seats on the hospital board that you can stop homicides in your hospital.

In the area my family lives in, the vast majority of Christians refuse to be treated in the only hospital that performs abortions. There are several hospitals to choose from, and a boycott of the "death" hospital may eventually have some effect. It is good to boycott such a hospital for all purposes, but it's especially effective to refuse to go to such hospitals to give birth.

Christian women may also decide not to seek ob-gyn care from any doctor who performs abortions. Find out also if your doctor will refer his patients to seek abortions from another colleague. That is additional grounds for finding a new doctor.

Doctors who perform abortions are often some of the sloppiest doctors around. I once worked on a case where a doctor botched the abortion of a baby whose mother was twelve years old. The girl was so badly ripped up that another doctor had to perform a hysterectomy and a colostomy just to save the girl's life. If such cases come to light in your area, you can demand that the state medical association revoke the license of such doctors.

Christian lawyers who specialize in medical malpractice will be more than willing to sue a doctor for a botched abortion or other substandard medical care. Financial pressure on their insurance companies can sometimes put these butchers out of business.

Christian Action Council does an outstanding job of establishing and training local people to operate crisis pregnancy centers. Your voluntary support of these centers in the form of both time and money will save countless lives.

Finally, I would urge parents and churches to make sure

our young people are so thoroughly committed to the pro-life principles that they will have the opportunity to counsel their acquaintances not to seek abortion as a solution to an unwanted pregnancy. It is naive to assume that girls in our churches will never find themselves in this position.

Drug and Alcohol Abuse

As a teenager in the late sixties and early seventies, I was aware that a few of my acquaintances were using drugs or alcohol. A recent survey in my county indicated that over 75 percent of the high school students use alcohol or drugs on a monthly basis. The situation has gotten worse because society tolerates these abuses.

If we deplore drug abuse generally, why do we seem to tolerate those whom we know are selling and using illegal drugs?

At the heart of the solution to the drug crisis is a personal willingness to refuse to tolerate any illegal use of drugs. If there are drug dealers in your neighborhood, report them. Call the police and insist that they stop such sales. Usually, your identity will not be revealed. Ask the police about this if you are concerned. I believe that at least one law-abiding citizen in every community in the country knows about most of the people selling and abusing drugs. A substantial decrease in such activity would occur if all Americans acted on the knowledge they have.

We need to teach our children that drug and alcohol use will destroy their lives. We need to teach them both in word and in deed. Too many Christians have developed softer attitudes toward excessive alcohol use in recent years. I have a hard time with the idea that we can engage in an activity and yet expect our children to abstain from that same conduct.

Pornography

Some time ago, a television station in Tacoma, Washington, aired a movie that contained a scene featuring frontal male nudity. This movie was full of filthy language and vulgarity. This was a regular television station, not cable. I contacted all of the advertisers whose ads appeared on that program, asking them to contact the station and tell the station manager that they would never permit their ads to be shown on such a program again. About half the advertisers responded favorably. Some responded negatively, and some did not respond at all.

I published the results of my project in a Christian newspaper that was circulated statewide. I asked people to write to the advertisers to tell them that if they didn't join in our campaign for better television, we would boycott their products.

We did not succeed in changing every company's position. But one company in particular learned the hard way that you cannot ignore Christian citizens who choose to spend their money with morally responsible businesses. A glass company had a bid for a $60,000 job on a church that had been through a major fire. This glass company lost the job and the church informed them that the company's failure to support our position was the reason they chose a different company. The company president called to inform me that he was changing his views.

That project took me about ten hours of time. Anyone could do what I did. Focus on the Family has assisted a network of state organizations that publish newsletters like the one I had in Washington at that time. (See Appendix for addresses.) Remember, I was dealing with a local television show and local advertisers. This was not a national boycott. Generally, every television show has both local and national sponsors. The networks sell the national ads and the local station sells the local ads. Don Wildmon's American Family Association is on the front line on national boycotts. You can effectively help by dealing with local advertisers whose ads appear on inappropriate shows.

There are several things you can do to combat the sale of soft-core pornography. You will remember the successful campaign to boycott 7-11 stores until they removed *Playboy, Penthouse,* and other magazines. You can do the same thing if there are grocery, drug, or convenience stores in your area that sell these magazines.

Contact a number of churches in your area asking them to place notices in their bulletins of stores that sell such magazines. You could write a letter to the owners or managers of those stores asking them to remove such magazines. Your letter will gain additional significance if a number of others sign, especially lay and church leaders. If there is no appropriate response, simply publicize your right to take your business elsewhere.

Let every compatible church in your area know of the project and you will usually get amazing cooperation. There are a lot of people willing to join such a project; the usual lack is leadership. If you are willing to make a few calls, write a couple of letters, and follow through with churches, you can really help clean up the family stores in your community.

Finally, you can be successful in addressing the issue of hard-core pornography. There are good laws on the books in almost every state. There are excellent federal laws outlawing hard-core pornography. The main reason there still are adult theaters, bookstores, and peep-show outlets is that the prosecuting attorney simply hasn't taken action. Most of these prosecutors would be willing to act if they felt they had community support.

Circulate a petition to every church in your area. Ask your local prosecutor (in some states they are called district attorneys, or state's attorneys) to fully prosecute every potential violation of the state's obscenity laws. Also address your petition to the U.S. attorney for your area.

These prosecutors are usually elected officials. And they know that if they begin to prosecute obscenity cases, they are going to face attacks by the ACLU, the press, and liberal politicians. They need to know that a great number of average citizens support them.

It is really not that difficult to obtain 5,000 or more signatures on a petition if you live in an area of any significant population. And let me tell you that there are very few prosecutors who would fail to respond to a petition signed by even 200 people. Give them some political support and they will usually take steps to clean up your community.

Homosexuality

If you understand the legal theory of a gay rights law, you will be able to effectively argue against such a law if it becomes an issue in your state or community.

As a general rule an employer can hire anyone he wants. A landlord is able to rent to a person of his own choosing. If an employer doesn't want to hire someone because the person graduated from Harvard and not Yale, that is the employer's right. It's a free country and he can do what he pleases. The basis for this rule is a strong belief in freedom.

But there are exceptions to this general rule of freedom. We have decided as a nation that some things are so important that we are willing to give up a little of our freedom to achieve other goals. We have decided, for instance, that racial equality is so important we've given up our "freedom" to discriminate against another person on the basis of race. That decision is a good one and widely supported by the American people. We have similar laws banning discrimination on the basis of gender, national origin, or religion. Again, our belief in the importance of these principles is enough to say we are willing to forfeit a little freedom to achieve these other goals.

These protective laws really do give special legal protection to people because of their race, gender, national origin, and religion. These are special protections not available to people who are discriminated against because of their educational background, sloppy grammar, poor handwriting, personal habits, etc. We are willing to sacrifice some freedom for racial equality, but not for the protection of those with poor penmanship.

For a gay rights law, we have to ask ourselves: Is homosexuality so important that we are willing to sacrifice our freedom to grant special protection to homosexuality? I don't think so. Why should we lose our freedom to advance their choice of sexual practices? Racial harmony is good for the nation and worthy of some sacrifices. Homosexuality cannot be construed to be good for our nation.

This does not mean that homosexuals should not have rights as *individuals*. On the contrary, they should have equal rights with everyone. But, their rights must stem from the fact that they are citizens, not from the fact that they are homosexuals. Gay rights laws seek greater protection than what is granted to other citizens.

You should speak up in your community if such a law is ever proposed. Homosexuals shouldn't be allowed to marry each other, adopt children, or demand other special privileges that would come from such laws.

Local citizen groups have been overwhelmingly successful in stopping gay rights laws in a number of cities.

Divorce

Let me write very briefly about this subject. Easy divorce has done immeasurable damage to millions of children in this nation. And we know that children who come from divorced homes are much more likely to end up in divorce than those raised in homes with intact marriages.

I have been in a number of churches where divorce was readily accepted as a way of life. To me, this is a dangerous *attitude,* even though divorce is not the unpardonable sin, and we should not treat divorced people in our churches as lepers. I would strongly encourage those who have been divorced, however, to give a strong testimony of warning to others against divorce and its long-term consequences.

I remember handling a legal matter for a Christian woman who had been divorced. Her husband was active in the choir and had an affair with the woman who was the choir director. He divorced his wife and married the other woman.

In the midst of this legal dispute, a community Christian choir performed in our church. This husband and his new wife performed in the choir. Not only did they sing, but the choir shared testimonies. I was absolutely appalled when this man began sharing his testimony of how God had led him to find a new wonderful wife who was so fulfilling. He didn't mention that she was half the age of his first wife and about the age of his oldest child whom he'd abandoned.

God did not lead this man into adultery and divorce. If people with troubled marriages hear testimonies like the one

I heard, they will be tempted to believe that divorce may be God's will for them too.

If we want America's families to remain intact, let's be sure that the life messages we hear *in our churches* promote fidelity.

The Rights and Risks of Engaging in Public Activism

Operation Rescue has served to bring a national awareness to two problems: first, abortion; second, the fact that there are risks in taking a stand for moral righteousness. At the outset, some involved in Operation Rescue activities seemed to believe they would suffer no consequences for breaking the law, since the moral correctness of their objective is so obvious. But, that hope has dissipated in the light of the tremendous bias the legal system has against those who oppose abortion.

Operation Rescue is controversial, even within the Christian community. Some people believe that those who engage in rescues are justified in breaking the trespassing laws in order to save babies from execution. Others believe that there are legal methods to accomplish the same objective. There can be no doubt on one point: The police brutality and stiff sentences that have been meted out upon those engaging in rescues is severe. We would have to return to Vietnam protests in Chicago during the 1968 Democratic National Convention and Kent State to find anything to parallel the fierceness of the reaction being received by participants of Operation Rescue.

I have no intention of debating the validity of Operation Rescue, or of describing the rights of those who engage in that kind of political activity. By discussing the rights and risks of public activism, I intend to deal with only those kinds of activities that are clearly legal. Even when we stick clearly within the law, however, there are risks involved. Thanks to our founding fathers, our legal system does recognize that we have rights. Let's consider the three most likely risks you may face and steps to protect your rights for each.

1. *Unwanted personal publicity.* If you engage in a public stand for righteousness, you become a public personality. The more visible your action and the more controversial your position, the more the media will want to know about you. You may also find yourself receiving unwanted phone calls and other contacts at home. (Let me suggest that you may receive unwanted phone calls from friends and foes alike.)

Before engaging in high-profile public activism, be sure to talk this over with your family. They will not escape from the spotlight. You may want to consider getting an unlisted phone number as well as take other precautions to protect your family's privacy.

2. *Threats from government officials.* If you are gathering signatures for a petition or initiative, you may find that some government officials may not like it. They may do to you what once happened to me in Spokane, and call the police to try to stop you. You have a clear-cut constitutional right to "petition the government for redress of grievances." If the police try to stop you from using a public sidewalk for political purposes, they are violating your civil rights. *You should contact one of the legal groups listed in the Appendix.*

The best response to any other kind of threat issued by a government official is to simply inform the media of the threat. The public is entitled to know if they have government officials who have decided to act like bullies.

3. *Threats of lawsuits.* The kind of lawsuit you are most likely to face as a result of public activism is a suit for libel or slander. Keep in mind that truth is always an absolute defense to such suits. It is not a defense that someone else told you the questionable information. If you say it in public you are responsible for the validity of the information.

The rules I have just stated are the rules that apply to the slander of a private individual. There are different rules for slander of a public figure. Any elected official is a public figure. Any person who regularly gets his name in the newspaper is also a public figure. You may become a public figure by taking a visible stand.

If you say something about a public figure, you can only be held liable if (1) you say something you know is false; or

(2) you say something with reckless disregard of whether it is true or false. If you take reasonable steps to check out the truth of a matter, you will not have any legal trouble from a lawsuit from a public figure, even if it turns out that the information you were given was not precisely accurate.

The Benefits of Public Activism

Over the past fifteen years, I have faced each of the different risks of public activism we have just reviewed—and more. If you behave responsibly there is very little chance that any of the threats will ever materialize. Even if people threaten, it is my experience that they rarely follow through.

My overall purpose of including this discussion of risks was to help focus attention on the need to count the costs of taking a stand. Yes, there are risks and other costs; but I have found that God is a faithful and mighty Defender of those who are standing for Him in accordance with His principles.

Just as in any other area of Christian service, there are costs involved. But if we fail to follow the *leading of God* when He asks us to take a stand for the right, we will lose far more than man can ever take from us. We lose the thrill of seeing God work in our lives. We lose the blessing that comes from remaining in the center of God's will for our lives. And we lose the heritage of righteousness that we could help to establish for the benefit of our children and grandchildren.

I, for one, am convinced that the benefits of taking a stand more than compensate for the risks and burdens.

◇ **12** ◇

The Global Battle for Religious Freedom

The collapse of communism in the Soviet Union and in Eastern Europe has radically changed our view of religious freedom in those countries. There is a new and profound openness to God in many of these countries—at least for now. But there are many other parts of the world where Christianity is under attack.

For the next decade it would appear that nations under Islamic rule pose the greatest threat to religious liberty for Christians and others who value religious freedom. We must remember that atheistic communism still controls China, the most populous nation on earth. The lessons we learned in the battle for religious freedom behind the Iron Curtain can serve as the blueprint for the years ahead as the threat of religious repression surfaces in new areas of the world.

On November 14, 1980, Vladimir Khailo was summarily arrested by the Soviet KGB. Pastor Khailo, a Ukrainian Baptist evangelist, was arrested as a result of work with the underground Baptist churches in the Soviet Union.

Khailo was tried in the system euphemistically called "Soviet Justice." All his church work was clearly grounds for the Communist system to want to crush this man. They decided, however, that Khailo was really not "a criminal"; rather, he was "sick." He was "diagnosed" by Soviet psychiatrists as a "religious schizophrenic" and sentenced to a Soviet mental hospital. Khailo later described the hospital as "a prison within a prison."

In addition to his religious activity, the Communists pointed to the fact that he and his wife had fifteen children as further "evidence" of his mental illness. Unlike their American counterparts, Soviet Christians routinely have very large families.

For six and a half years, the Communists tried every imaginable form of "treatment" to break this courageous man's will and get him to renounce Christianity. Though battered and bruised, Khailo refused to renounce his Lord.

At times, Khailo felt alone and forgotten, but there were a committed group of Christians in the West who refused to let Khailo's situation become another statistic of Soviet cruelty.

Christian Solidarity International (CSI) was founded in 1977 by Hans-Jurg Stuckelburg, a pastor from Zurich, Switzerland. Pastor Stuckelburg was moved by the fact that many organizations were speaking regularly for Soviet Jews who were undergoing severe persecution, but no one appeared to be speaking for Soviet Christians like Khailo.

CSI launched a campaign for Khailo both in the United States and Europe. Letters were written to Soviet officials demanding his release. Calls and letters were sent to American officials asking for their assistance in pressing the case of Vladimir Khailo with Soviet officials.

One American official who undertook steps of intervention in response to CSI's requests was Republican Congressman Frank Wolf of Virginia. Wolf undertook intensive efforts to urge the release of Pastor Khailo.

In the meantime the Soviet officials had other ideas for this man. They had decided that after six and a half years in the psychiatric hospital, they were not going to be able to break his will. On March 17, 1987, Khailo was directed out into a parking area in the hospital compound, where he was shaken to the core with what he saw. A vehicle known as "the black van" was there to transport him to another location. This van was there to take him to his death.

While standing in the hospital-prison yard, a messenger arrived delivering an order to the officials in charge of Khailo. The directive had come from Moscow: Release Vladimir

Khailo. Khailo was so overcome with astonishment and relief that he fainted. When he came to, they confirmed that the order was true: He was to be a free man!

Congressman Wolf played a key role in the next stage of Khailo's bid for freedom. After intensive efforts and negotiations, Khailo, his wife, ten of their children, five grandchildren, two sons-in-law and one daughter-in-law were granted permission to emigrate to the United States. On January 19, 1988, the Khailo family landed at Chicago's O'Hare Airport and began living as a family in freedom for the first time in their lives. At the time, it was the largest family ever permitted to leave the Soviet Union.

The prayers, calls, and letters offered up by Christians in the West, together with the political efforts inspired by CSI, had been used by God. But make no mistake—it was a miracle from the Lord that this family was set free.

A Firsthand Look at Communist Repression of Christians

In July of 1988, I went to the Soviet Union as a part of a CSI delegation to seek freedom for other Soviet Christians. The year before, I had been elected chairman of the United States division of CSI. The delegation included Rep. Frank Wolf and David Amess, a member of Parliament in Great Britain.

We visited Soviet Christians who had recently been released from prison. Gleb Yakunin, a Russian Orthodox priest, invited us into his living room to tell us of his experience in Soviet prisons and the ongoing needs of Christians in his country. I'll never forget the series of homemade locks on the front door of his apartment. Clearly they had been needed, but equally clear was the fact that they had been no match for the abilities and ruthlessness of the KGB.

We also visited the 25th-floor apartment of Galena Baratz. Galena was a middle-aged woman who had been a college professor. Her husband had been an official in the Soviet Air Force. Both of their careers were terminated when they accepted Jesus as their Savior. Galena had been given a new job as a street sweeper.

I had heard about Galena's story before we arrived in Moscow and how she had been ordered to be a street sweeper. But it wasn't until I saw a street sweeper on the streets of Moscow that I understood the deep cruelty involved in this career demotion.

Throughout Moscow, I saw old women standing along the edge or sometimes in the middle of major urban thoroughfares, the American equivalent of an eight-lane highway. Traffic was whizzing by at unbelievable speeds that would terrify most American drivers. In America, these streets would be cleaned from time to time. But the equipment would be heavy trucks with spraying water and rotating brushes. In Moscow, the equipment was old women with a bundle of sticks, one long stick and a number of small switches of wood tied to the handle—a broom straight out of the middle ages.

The street sweepers in Moscow could not possibly clean the streets. Their weapons were too ancient to battle modern filth (and filthy it was). The sole apparent purpose for this position was to humiliate women like Mrs. Baratz.

When we were in Moscow, Galena was under *de facto* house arrest. She was living in an apartment belonging to a young couple with two young children. The KGB was trying to starve this family out of their home by refusing to let anyone in or out of the apartment. Food had been brought in by lowering a basket from their apartment window to a neighboring apartment's balcony. We were able to go to a grocery store reserved for diplomats and other foreigners. The food there was much better and more plentiful than could be purchased by Soviet citizens. We bought Galena and her host family $150 worth of groceries and walked past the KGB guards. It helps to have a member of the British Parliament with you when you are trying such tactics.

Our delegation had several meetings with Soviet officials in which we demanded the release of Christians from prison and the psychiatric hospitals. I had a special meeting where I met with Soviet lawyers who were rewriting the Soviet law on "religious freedom." At that meeting I had the opportunity to demand that they allow religious freedom for children. I sought the right to have Sunday schools, Christian schools, and home schools for Soviet Christians—all of which were prohibited at the time. Even before the collapse of the Soviet system, some of these reforms were allowed in the months that followed.

Western Christians Can Help

The efforts of Christians from the West really can have a major impact on foreign governments. Consider the following letter written to Christian Solidarity International by Alexander Ogorodnikov, a Russian whom we met in Moscow shortly after he had been released from prison. His "crime" had been holding Christian meetings for teenagers.

July 21, 1988

Dear Brothers and Sisters!

We wish to thank you all for your activities in defending the ideals of freedom of religion and in restoring the degraded human dignity.

Your prayers cut through barbed wire and penetrated the huge dark prison walls, instilling hope into desperate hearts. Your efforts generate active Christian solidarity, teaching a lesson in lofty morals to a world beset by separation, loneliness, and indifference. We, the Russian Christians, bow before you in gratitude for your many years of struggle to defend the prisoners of conscience. Despite the resistance of the power state machinery, this struggle will be successful. We thank you for your prayers and for acting as spokesmen on our behalf, on behalf of the silenced, thus taking away at least part of the accusation of cowardly silence. You passed on our names to the believers everywhere and now that we return home from captivity, we send you, brothers and sisters, words of sincere appreciation and love.

Christian solidarity knows no boundaries. Though we may be separated by watchtowers, the Iron Curtain, the six-meter-high Berlin wall, the strict censorship of correspondence, the kalasmikoffs, and the barking of cruel shepherd dogs, yet we hope that these obstacles will not deter brotherly love. Your organization's activity is a worthy example.

We are praying for you. May the Lord bless you in your noble work on behalf of truth and Christian solidarity.

Lovingly,
Alexander Ogorodnikov
Moscow

Freedom Triumphs in Romania

Intervention by Christians in the West can indeed help free our Christian brothers and sisters from atheistic and other oppressive regimes. CSI was deeply involved in the press for religious freedom in Romania. It sponsored several trips for United States congressmen to demonstrate the nature of the abuse of the Ceausecu Communist dictatorship. Prior to CSI's efforts, the State Department had succeeded in granting special economic favors to Romania because Ceausecu was seen as independent from Moscow. Christians understood that Ceausecu was nothing more than a rogue—independent from Moscow, yes somewhat—but he remained a brutal Communist oppressor.

Representative Frank Wolf was one of those who traveled to Romania with CSI. Ceausecu was so bold that he ordered his soldiers to march Congressman Wolf down the street away from the door of a persecuted believer with machine guns pointed at his back. Wolf did not back down. When he returned to Congress he worked together with Senator Bill Armstrong to eliminate the special economic favors our country was giving to Romania. Experts believe that this economic move was a significant factor in speeding the demise of communism in that country.

Paul Negrut, co-pastor of Oradea Baptist Church, the largest Baptist church not only in Romania but in all of Europe, now serves with me on CSI's international board of directors. Pastor Negrut has told me two things that are really important for American Christians to understand. First, he has emphasized the importance of the significant help that Christians from free countries can be to Christians who are suffering oppression. He said, "CSI has served as an umbrella of protection over churches and individuals. The reason I am not dead is because of the grace of God and the help of Christians in the West." Second, he warns that just because the Communist regimes have fallen, we should not assume that religious freedom is on solid ground in former Communist countries like Romania. He points out that many people who were Communist officials in the old Department of Cults are now serving as officials in the new Ministry of Religious Affairs.

The truth is that we may not know for several years how the quest for freedom will turn out in these countries. And we must remain vigilant for religious liberty on behalf of those who have suffered so much for our Lord.

Oppression in Nepal

Communist countries are not the only enemies of Christians. Hindu and Muslim countries can be violent oppressors of those who profess faith in the Lord Jesus Christ.

One country that has had a record of serious oppression of Christians is the Hindu nation of Nepal.

In November of 1989, Nepalese police disrupted a church service outside the capital city of Kathmandu. All the believers present were arrested and beaten. They were then forced to worship before a Hindu idol. Only seven women and their seventy-five-year-old pastor refused to bow before the idol.

Shortly after this incident, the police arrested Charles Mendies. Mendies is an evangelist who also runs an orphanage for fifty children. He was arrested for "proselytizing." Mendies was beaten and his wife and three children were threatened in an attempt to intimidate other Christians.

Mengale Pakhring was a Buddhist who converted to Christianity. He was badly beaten and then arrested. He was kept in solitary confinement and continued to be beaten in an effort to get him to recant his faith in Christ. He refused.

CSI took a delegation to Nepal in May of 1990. Our people met with Prime Minister Bhattarai and presented him with a list of twenty-nine Christians we wanted freed from Nepalese prisons. Just eighteen days later, King Birenda, acting on the advice of the Prime Minister, granted amnesty for all religious prisoners and ordered their release.

The Threat to Christian Minorities in the Muslim World

Muslim nations perhaps represent the most significant threat to the safety and liberty of Christians at this juncture of world history. Consider what we know from a Muslim nation that is considered somewhat friendly and open in the West—Egypt.

In early 1991, three young men in their twenties were all arrested after they gave their testimony of conversion to Christianity in a Presbyterian church just outside of Cairo. Mustafa Mohammad Said all-Shargawi, Sallam Hussein Mohammad Ibrahim, and Hass Mohammad Ismai'l Mohammad were charged with "conducting actions against a heavenly religion (Islam)" and "disturbing the social peace." They continued to be detained even after the court had initially found them not guilty.

CSI and other human rights organizations were able to present this case to Senator Jesse Helms, who took the matter to the United States Senate. He was rapidly gaining support for official response to the denial of human rights in Egypt when the court suddenly dismissed the charges and released the three Christian men.

Egypt's Coptic Christians are a significant minority in that nation. They suffer persecution, discrimination, beatings, and arrests on a regular basis there. Often the actions are at the hands of Islamic extremists rather than the government, but the government's failure to prosecute and punish violators together with a consistent pro-Islamic position in the state-controlled press tends to support this kind of oppression.

This is what we know from a relatively open Muslim country. The situation is undoubtedly worse in a number of Islamic nations that are more secretive and closed to the

West. A pastor from Malaysia, who for security reasons should not be named in this book, told me story after story of the severe and violent persecution that befalls Christian converts in this heavily Muslim nation.

Communism Continues to Threaten Christians

We do need to remember that despite the fall of communism in eastern Europe, this atheistic system continues to hold sway in a number of other nations. Chinese Pastor Zhang Yongliang was recently sentenced to three years in prison for illegal preaching. I have had the privilege of meeting Caleb Mesa, an evangelical pastor from Peru. In his nation, the Communist guerrillas control significant parts of the nation. They recently murdered a number of evangelical pastors, including American workers with World Vision.

We can take some important steps of action to help draw a line of protection around our Christian brothers and sisters who are suffering under such regimes.

1. We need to get a steady flow of accurate information about persecuted Christians. I know of no better source than Christian Solidarity International. You can get their free newsletter by writing to CSI, P.O. Box 70563, Washington, D.C. 20024.
2. We need to write letters of encouragement to persecuted Christians in the cases where it is safe to write.
3. We need to write letters to officials of offending nations demanding safe treatment, release and religious liberty for Christians.
4. We need to keep pressure on our State Department by writing to the White House, urging that our foreign policy consistently takes a position linking our nation's favor with a positive record on human rights—particularly religious freedom.
5. We need to write letters of encouragement and support to those leaders in the Congress and Senate who stand up for the rights of those persecuted for their faith.
6. We need to regularly pray for persecuted Christians, by name if possible.

7. Finally, we need to exhibit the kind of courage I saw displayed by a Soviet believer in the following story, whom I met when I was in Moscow in 1988.

The first Sunday we were there we attended First Baptist Church of Moscow. The church would have seated 400 or 500 in the United States. I would estimate that 1500 Christians were jammed into this facility and standing on the street listening intently to the speakers. Eighty percent of those in attendance were older women. There were very few men at all, and almost no men of my age (30's to 40's).

After the service a man about my age came up to me and said what sounded like "Roosky Biblios." I didn't speak any Russian and he didn't speak any English, but I understood that he wanted a Russian Bible. Through crude sign language and some letters I drew in the back of my own Bible, I was able to communicate to him that I would meet him at 2:00 P.M. at the subway station across the street from my hotel.

I showed up with the Bible wrapped inside an American T-shirt. He didn't want to be seen getting the Bible in public, so he and I went off into the woods about a hundred fifty yards from the subway station. I laid the Bible on the ground, pretended to tie my shoe, and then left the Bible there as I took off in the opposite direction. He took the Bible and left.

It was obvious that he was scared. And though objectively I had little to be frightened of, I admit that I was scared at the time as well. His fear was reasonable and genuine. However, upon reflection I believe that he exemplified the true meaning of the word *courage.* Courage is not fearlessness. Courage means doing what is right even when you have good reason to be afraid.

Christians in many nations are called upon to act with this kind of courage on an almost daily basis. We need to act courageously in our support for them.

13

Becoming a Wise Voter

Christians get very excited whenever we hear a candidate for political office say anything about God. We are so hungry for people who share our values we often will blindly follow a person who makes even a vague reference to the Bible or Christian principles. I have heard conversations that go something like this:

"Are you going to vote for Thompson or Stevens for state legislature this year?"

"I like Thompson. The other day on the radio I heard him say that 'God helps those who help themselves.' He must be a Christian to say something like that in public."

In this scenario it is just as likely that Thompson is pro-abortion and pro-gay rights—substantive positions that should cause any Christian to *refrain* from siding with the candidate. Christians need to have a greater degree of practical wisdom in assessing which candidates deserve our support.

Voting is important for all of us. In fact, one of the most important ways we can "draw the line" between right and wrong is by standing in line to cast our vote. Most people have very little understanding about the candidates for whom they eventually cast their ballot. An intelligent voter is the most dangerous "enemy" feared by many politicians.

It is very important for us to be good stewards of all that God has given us. Our duty to be good stewards includes our rights as citizens to elect the leaders who will govern our community, state, and nation. A wise voter is one who understands the office to be filled, has determined what issues are relevant to the office, and has discovered what the candidates believe on each of these relevant issues. A *really* wise voter shares this information with other citizens and thereby influences the outcome of the election in a significant manner.

This is a lot easier than it sounds. In fact, what we most need to appropriate is godly common sense. The woman described in Proverbs 31 was a very spiritual woman, but she also had extraordinary practical skills and abundant good sense. One of the attributes of the godly woman was that her husband "sat in the gate," which means that he was a ruler in the city. We can see more people who share our values "sitting in the city gates" all over our nation if we take a little time to wisely determine how we should vote.

A Little "Homework"

1. *Understand the office.*

In some elections, you'll be electing candidates for a dozen or more different offices. If you want to vote intelligently, you need to have some idea of the responsibilities and duties that go with each of these offices. The duties of a United States congressman are totally different than the duties of a member of the County Board of Supervisors. Therefore, both the qualifications and, more important, the issues you focus on for each office will vary greatly.

If you have any doubt what duties the office entails, call the current office holder and simply ask a staff member to explain the duties and responsibilities of the office. Your local Republican or Democratic committee is also a good source of information. A reference librarian at your library could also steer you to information on the duties of a particular office. You may not know what the duties are of the state commissioner of public lands or the state treasurer, but if you are going to vote for these positions, ten to fifteen minutes of reading will teach you enough about the responsibilities of the offices to last for a lifetime of elections.

2. *Determine which issues are relevant.*

The most important decision you can ever make about voting is the decision to choose candidates based on the positions they take on issues—not on personalities or solely on party affiliation. If candidates understand that they are going to earn our votes only by taking proper stands on important issues, it will go a long way toward changing some of the problems we are experiencing in the political process.

As important as the issue of abortion is, for example, there are some offices for which this is really not the best issue to focus on in discerning the candidates with good positions from those with bad positions. You need to be able to match the issues with the office being sought. For instance, a candidate's position on balancing the federal budget is simply not relevant in deciding who should sit on your school board.

Let me say just a word about the relevance of party affiliation. The very first vote cast by a member of a state legislature or Congress will be for officers of the House and Senate. The 1991 hearings on Clarence Thomas emphasized that there is a substantial difference between Senator Joseph Biden and Senator Orrin Hatch. When the Republicans were in control of the Senate, Hatch was the chairman of the committee. Biden is chairman when the Democrats are in the majority. Though many of us don't think in these terms, a vote for a Republican or a Democrat in a race for a U.S. Senate seat to represent your home state has an effect "upstream." It actually affects the outcome of the race between Biden and Hatch for the chairmanship of the Senate Judiciary Committee. In that sense, voting by party affiliation is an important issue, but it's only one issue to be weighed with other factors. It will not override, for example, a candidate's view on abortion.

When you begin thinking about a candidate's stand on issues, you need to start thinking in terms of questions that will clearly identify the likely voting pattern the candidate will follow once he or she is in office. "Believe it or not," some political candidates might equivocate on issues to try to confuse voters. My favorite political-equivocation line is: "Some of my friends are for that issue. Some of my friends are opposed. I stand with my friends."

In order to stop candidates from being able to successfully waffle like this, learn to ask precise questions.

Let me share some examples, matched to a number of particular offices.

City Council / County Board of Supervisors

Gay rights is an issue likely to surface in city politics. The question you ask should be phrased in the way the legislation is likely to be written.

- Will you oppose a bill prohibiting discrimination on the basis of sexual orientation?

Zoning for churches is an issue that is exclusively determined by local government.

- Will you support a lenient application of the zoning laws so that churches can easily be established and expanded in our city?

Sheriff

Law enforcement issues are often overlooked but are important to Christians.

- Will you vigorously enforce all laws against pornography in our county?
- Will you vigorously enforce all laws against prostitution and sodomy in our county?

State Legislature

There are always at least a dozen or more good questions that can be asked candidates for the state legislature on issues from taxes and spending to civil rights and religious freedom. Here are just a few examples.

- Will you support legislation to preclude abortions except to save the life of the mother?
- Will you oppose any government funding of abortion or abortion counseling?
- Will you support legislation to allow home schools and

private schools to be free from government interference?

- Will you oppose any legislation that bans discrimination on the basis of sexual orientation?
- Will you oppose any increase in state taxes?

Attorney General

In many states the attorney general is an elected position. This position is often overlooked, but it can be very influential. A local Christian lawyer could help you draft questions that would be pertinent to the race at the time of the election. Here are a few suggestions.

- Will you assist local prosecutors with vigorous state-wide prosecution of obscenity?
- Do you believe that it is unconstitutional to tax churches?
- Will you advise the state agency handling child-abuse complaints that moderate corporal punishment is not child abuse, and therefore should not be grounds for child-abuse investigations?

President, United States Senate, Congress

Good questions to ask candidates for federal office include:

- Will you support an amendment to require a balanced federal budget?
- Will you refuse to support an unbalanced budget for the next fiscal year?
- Will you vote to support a "right to life" amendment to the Constitution?
- Will you vote to prohibit any federal funding of abortion?
- Will you oppose the addition of "sexual orientation" to federal civil rights laws? (This phrase is the legal terminology for gay rights legislation.)

3. *Find out where the candidates stand on the issues of importance to you.*

Candidates are only too eager to tell you where they stand
on issues of importance to them. But many candidates go into
an election with a game plan of avoiding certain controversial
issues that may cost them votes. Often, those controversial
issues are the ones Christians would find the most important
in determining how to vote.

The best way to find out where a candidate stands on
issues is to simply write him or her a letter and ask for specific
answers. It's unlikely that a single citizen or a local group
will get a presidential candidate to answer a series of questions that you send in a letter. If you are properly organized,
however, you will probably get responses from candidates
for Congress and perhaps even the United States Senate.

The first time I ever tried to create a survey was in 1980.
By linking a large number of churches together who were
willing to pass out the results, we were able to get personal
interviews with every candidate for governor, one candidate
for the United States Senate, a number of congressmen and
the majority of the state legislative candidates. Incidentally,
the candidate for the U.S. Senate who answered our questionnaire defeated a long-term incumbent. Our survey did
not "deliver" his victory, but there is little question that we
reached at least 5 to 7 percent of the state electorate, and this
had some positive impact on his candidacy.

Here is one example of the process of creating a "candidates survey," using a city council election as an illustration.
Let's assume that there are seven different districts within
the city, with one council seat for each district.

First, form a small committee of citizens who will be responsible for the candidates survey. Ideally you would have
seven members of your committee, one from each district in
the city. Try to get one or two prominent citizens to serve on
your committee. But the real work of such projects usually
falls into the laps of people who can truly be called "average
citizens."

Second, agree upon a list of questions that you think are
the most important for the office. Seven to ten questions are

a good number. Be sure that each question is worded in such a way as to permit a yes or no answer. Candidates will often want to add a brief explanation and that is acceptable as well.

Third, mail the questionnaire to every candidate. Do not mail only to candidates of one party. Even if there are independent or obscure parties involved, mail your questionnaire to every single candidate. Make sure that you inform the candidates that you need their responses by a certain deadline and that you will publish their responses.

Fourth, publish the candidates' responses. You will avoid all kinds of legal problems if you follow these simple rules in publishing:

1. Never endorse any candidate in this publication.
2. Do not "score" candidates 100 percent or 50 percent or any other scoring system. Simply state the candidates' answers.
3. Do not indicate a position on the issues. For example, do not indicate that the correct answer to question three is yes. If Christian voters receive information that Candidate A is in favor of gay rights and Candidate B is opposed to gay rights, you do not have to tell them which is the better position on that issue.

Fifth, circulate the responses to as many churches throughout the city as will take them. Distribute them to individuals and businesses that would like them as well. Another way to circulate this information is to get yourself invited to be a guest on a Christian radio talk show.

There is nothing illegal about circulating such material in church (including IRS rules), as long as you are careful to not endorse or oppose any candidate or group of candidates. As long as you are merely stating positions of candidates on issues without any editorial comment, you can proceed.

It would be a good idea to get a lawyer to review your plans in light of state election laws. If you cannot find or afford a lawyer, simply write the state election commission, set forth your plans step-by-step, and ask if there is any legal violation or registration requirement. It would also be a good idea to get a legal opinion about federal and IRS requirements, because these laws change and it is important that you get specific legal advice for your planned activities.

4. *Share your information with other voters.*

You will find Christians hungry for this kind of information. A half dozen mothers, or even a half dozen teenagers, could single-handedly create a voter's survey that would influence elections where over 100,000 ballots are cast. If you produce a one-page survey that can be reproduced by individual churches and have them inserted in church bulletins, you can influence tens of thousands of votes. Elections are often won or lost on very close margins. With ten to twenty (sometimes forty) hours of work, a half dozen people can help your community elect officials with views sympathetic to the Christian world view.

Very few have the knowledge to take on a task like this. Now you know what to do. If you can get a handful of friends to help, you can be a person who has helped draw a line of demarcation between those candidates worthy of your support and those who are not.

5. *Consider volunteer activity.*

With a few hours of time, you can help a candidate in a way that will have a great impact on the election. And if an issue should arise that you feel needs to be addressed after the election, campaign volunteers always will be given more serious consideration than people who have no connection with the candidate. Examples of some volunteer activity with limited time commitments are:

Telephone canvassing
Placing yard signs
Distributing literature
Hosting a meet-the-candidate coffee in your home

The Importance of a Single Vote

There are many examples of how elections are decided on very narrow margins. One recent example should cause us all to reflect soberly upon the importance of voting ourselves and to encourage others in our churches to do the same.

In the 1991 election in Washington State, there was an initiative on the ballot regarding abortion. Pro-abortion forces understood that the Supreme Court was in a position that could result in the reversal of *Roe* v. *Wade* at any time. They circulated a petition to place the right to an abortion into state law so that if *Roe* was reversed, allowing states to make their own decisions about abortion, a pro-abortion law would already be on the books.

The vote was very close. It was so close that a recount was required by state law. After the recount, the final vote to adopt this pro-abortion law was 756,812 voting yes and 752,590 voting no. There are 6,763 precincts in Washington State. It would have taken only one more no vote in 4,223 precincts to have changed the election. And there are more than 4,223 churches in the state. *One additional no vote per church would have stopped this pro-abortion law.*

If we use our rights as citizens to vote in a way that is consistent with our godly common sense, then the liberals can start writing books telling how they lost important elections by a single vote.

14

How to Be a "Citizen Lobbyist"

Politicians run for office promising to be "public servants." It is, therefore, up to the public to give our servants some directions on what we want done. Every elected official in the country can be influenced by calls and letters from his constituents. The number of people it takes to change his vote simply depends on the total amount of mail he gets on both sides of the issue, whether or not he has strong feelings about the particular bill, and whether somebody has given him campaign funds and is using this bill to cash in. If enough citizens write or call about a particular bill, average citizens can exert enough pressure to overcome the influence of paid lobbyists who use campaign money as bait.

There are approximately 600,000 people who live in most congressional districts. If just 100 of these people take the time to write to their representatives asking them to vote for a particular bill, they probably will. Every member of Congress takes a strong stand on a few issues, and on these issues it is much more difficult to sway his or her vote by letters or calls. But for the vast majority of bills coming before Congress, votes are up for grabs, depending on which side exerts the most pressure.

I use the term "citizen lobbyist" to describe a person who knows the steps of action necessary to exert influence on an elected official. It is really not that difficult. I saw an excellent anti-pornography bill pass through a state legislature even though there were more than a dozen professional lobbyists who were opposing the legislation. What made the difference? Thousands of average people—moms, dads, blue-collar workers, managers, homemakers, retirees—wrote a simple letter urging a favorable vote.

Here are the steps of action:

Lobbying Made Simple

1. *Get plugged into an organization that keeps track of legislation and notifies its members so that you know when to write.*

Most of us do not have time to keep track of what is going on in Congress or in our state legislatures. There are organizations that perform this watchdog service for you. For family, religious freedom, and abortion issues the very best groups in Washington, D.C., are Family Research Council, Concerned Women for America, and Coalitions for America. Coalitions for America has a new program that shows a great deal of promise. It is a once a month live program called *Library Court Live* beamed by satellite to a number of locations around the country. At this meeting activists from a great number of organizations and congressional leaders and staffers attend and share "action items" for important legislation in Congress. Family Research Council and Concerned Women for America perform similar functions through mailings, and each of them have access to radio. Family Research Council is an affiliate of Focus on the Family, the ministry of Dr. James Dobson. Beverly LaHaye, president of CWA, also has a daily radio program.

On the state level, Family Research Council has established a working relationship with a number of organizations. These groups perform "legislative watchdog" services in the state capitol. CWA also has state chapters in most states.

Then there are a number of excellent single-issue organizations. The best pro-life organization in my opinion is Christian Action Council. It has a strong biblical foundation and not only opposes abortion politically but has a vast network of crisis pregnancy centers that are designed to reach out to those with problem pregnancies and provide them realistic alternatives to abortion.

The Appendix of this book lists the addresses for all these groups and also lists several other fine organizations. I do not include any organization unless, from personal experience, I've observed effective action and integrity in the operation of the organization.

2. *Know what you are talking about.*

We covered this principle in an earlier chapter. As a brief reminder, it's critical that any contact you make with an elected official be a knowledgeable contact. If you've gotten information from a reputable organization, then step forward in confidence. And as we discussed earlier, there are other ways for you to verify facts yourself.

3. *When writing, refer to the bill by its bill number and, if possible, use the bill name.*

Legislative offices are very busy. Your letter will get much quicker attention if it has the bill number listed at the top of the letter. Your letter should be headed like this:

Date
The Honorable [Bill Smith]
United States Congress
Washington, D.C. 20515
Re: Support for H.R. 1234, The Parents Rights Bill
Dear Representative Smith,

By employing a heading like "Re: Support for H.B. 1234" or "Re: Opposition to S. 456," you immediately communicate your concern, and it shows that you really know what you are doing. Congressional aides like letters of this kind.

4. *Write a short, legible letter.*

A one-page handwritten or typed letter is ideal. Check your spelling. Use good penmanship. Do not jam your material so tightly on a page that it's hard to read.

I get a great volume of mail in my job as head of a national organization. If I get a long single-spaced letter I usually will not read it. My secretary will read it and tell me what it's about. And I can tell you that she's none too pleased with the assignment.

Legislators get far more mail than I do. If you want your letter to be read, make it brief, make it legible, and make it friendly. Simply state your position on the bill and give one or two reasons you feel the way you do.

5. *Ask for action.*

You should never write a legislator a letter without asking for specific steps of action that you want taken. "Vote against H.R. 1234," or "Become a co-sponsor of H.R. 2797," or "Introduce a bill protecting the rights of parents."

6. *Learn to respond to evasive answers.*

Representatives will sometimes write back, saying that they agree with your position and intend to take the action you requested. More infrequently, they will write back saying they disagree with your position. Most of the time you will get a letter which says something like this:

Dear Mrs. Jones,

Thank you for your letter concerning H.R. 1234, the Parents Rights Bill. Currently, this bill is before the Constitution Subcommittee of the Judiciary. Since I am not a member of this committee, my first opportunity to consider this legislation will be if and when this bill reaches the floor of the House.

At such time I will certainly take your views into consideration as I decide which way to vote on H.R. 1234.

Thank you so much for taking the time to share your views with me.

Sincerely,
Congressman Smith

This response letter is absolutely meaningless. But do not think that your letter will do no good. Before the vote the congressman will be told, "You have 67 letters in support of this bill and 12 letters in opposition." All things being equal, the side with the 67 letters will carry the day.

But there is a way to respond to evasive letters like the one we just read. You can write back:

Dear Congressman Smith,

I appreciate so much the time you took to write to me indicating that you would keep my views in mind when it comes time to vote for H.R. 1234, the Parents Rights Bill. However, I would deeply appreciate your support for this bill even before it reaches the floor of the House.

As you know, any Congressman can co-sponsor legislation, and this increases the political support for the bill, which increases its chances of reaching the floor of the House. Therefore, I urge you to co-sponsor this legislation at this time.

I believe this bill is of critical importance to the rights of parents to direct the upbringing of their children without unreasonable interference by the government.

You indicate that you will keep my views in mind when it comes time to vote for this bill. I appreciate that. However, I would also like to keep your views in mind when it comes time for me to vote for congressmen. I would deeply appreciate it if you would share those views with me.

> Sincerely,
> Mrs. Jones

7. *Personal visits work wonders.*

If you have the ability to visit an elected official in person, take the opportunity to do so. Remember that this man or woman is usually extremely busy so keep your remarks as brief as possible. A five to ten minute visit is the most you can usually expect. Therefore, after expressing thanks for the opportunity to visit, get to your point right away.

"We came today to ask for your support for H.B. 456, which will guarantee the rights of churches to control their own property. There are three reasons we support this bill. . . ."

If the official expands the time and goes further into the conversation that's fine. You should be prepared to make your points very quickly and succinctly.

8. *Become the personification of your issue.*

When I am training home-school leaders to become lobbyists for home education, I encourage them to get to know their state legislators. Visit them two to three times a year on a non-confrontational basis. Work in their campaign if possible. Give them even a small campaign contribution if you believe in their positions.

By getting to know one home-schooling family like this, a legislator will picture this family in his mind whenever it comes to voting on a bill about home schooling. He will think, "I'm voting for or against Mary and Bill." This is a very powerful position to be in, for such a legislator will find it extremely hard to vote against a person whom he knows in this way.

This same technique can be used for any other issue— crisis pregnancy centers, pornography, abortion, parents rights in public education, etc. If you become the individual best known to the legislator on that single issue and if you have taken the time to show that you are a thoughtful and responsible person, your letter or call to the legislator when it is time to vote will be extraordinarily influential.

The highly successful crusade "Mothers Against Drunk Driving" has been operated by ordinary citizens who have been extraordinarily successful in obtaining good legislation all across the nation. The liquor industry cannot compete with the effective technique of having average mothers cry out for protection for their children on the highways.

When a sufficient number of citizens care enough about an issue to become "citizen lobbyists," they can beat the special interest groups with their paid lobbyists nearly every time.

15

Working With "Our Friends" in the Media

The media is interested in controversy. Many of the types of disputes we have discussed will usually find their way into local newspapers, radio, and television. If you stand up for what is right, or if you are forced to defend your rights, there is a good chance you'll get a call from a reporter. If you believe that such a call is an opportunity rather than a threat, you may be able to effectively influence public opinion in your favor through the media.

Yes, there is some truth to the general idea that the media is controlled by the "left-wing establishment." Nonetheless, it's highly inappropriate for Christians to act as if the members of the media are our enemies. If you want to learn to deal with the media effectively, then the only time you should ever say "the media is all biased" is when you say it to yourself alone at home in your closet. We must get our message communicated to the public through the media; we do not have the option of ignoring the media or treating them as unapproachable enemies.

You *can* learn to effectively work with the media in a way that will maximize your opportunity to get your message to the public. So toss the "media is biased" mentality into the trash barrel and learn to deal effectively with this very influential part of American life.

Rebecca Hagelin, a public relations specialist from Vienna, Virginia, who represents numerous national Christian organizations, says, "Most Christians ignore the fact that the

Golden Rule applies to our relationships with people in the media too, often giving the press good cause to portray us in a negative light. If we are ever to hope for fair treatment by the media, it is the Christian's responsibility to break this vicious cycle and begin to operate under basic biblical guidelines, including being 'wise as a serpent, but gentle as a dove' in our dealings with reporters.''

General Principles for Good Media Relations

1. *Be truthful.*

We should be able to assume that Christians will tell the truth. But there is a tendency I've seen that has caused some good people to wind up in trouble with the media. This is the tendency to "fake it." If you are asked a question and you do not know the answer, never fake it. Simply say, "I don't know." If you make up a statistic that sounds right but you can't really remember or prove, then you're faking it. Do not succumb to this temptation.

Let's consider an example of a dispute with a local school district over a sex-education plan. If a reporter asks you, "How many parents are a part of your effort?"—do not succumb to the temptation to say, "Well, I am sure that hundreds of parents support what we are doing." That may be a good guess, but the proper truthful answer may be, "There are twelve parents who have been working together on this issue. However, we believe that a large number of others feel the same way." By this answer you have been entirely truthful, yet were able to make your basic point that in your opinion others feel as you do.

2. *Answer questions in a straightforward manner.*

Don't beat around the bush. If a reporter asks you a direct question, give a direct answer. It may be necessary to add some information that you want to get across, but that should follow your direct answer. If you do not answer questions straightforwardly, you will come off poorly, and as someone who doesn't deserve media coverage.

I'll never forget one horrible violation of this rule I observed personally. When I was in my early days of legal practice, there was a teachers' strike in our city. The court ruled that the strike was illegal, but the school district was not taking steps to enforce the court's ruling. A pastor and a small group asked me to intervene in the lawsuit so that their children could get back to school. We filed the legal papers and held a press conference on the steps of the courthouse. There were about twenty reporters present. One reporter addressed a question to the pastor, "How many people have joined this lawsuit?" This pastor launched into a five-minute history of his church and his fledgling television ministry and never did answer the reporter's question. By the time he finished, all the other reporters had left.

3. *Don't preach or over-spiritualize.*

Reporters are not used to King James English or church lingo, and we shouldn't use it in our communication with them. The most persuasive method of communication is to take your biblical ideas and learn to express them in words that can be understood by the media. Learn to guide your truths around their mental roadblocks.

One phrase should be avoided *at all costs*: Never accuse anyone of taking "satanic" action unless you are dealing with a self-proclaimed Satanist. If we are opposing someone whose actions are unbiblical, use words like wrong, erroneous, or ill-conceived. If you use the "sword"—Satan—the media will use your statement as an opportunity to destroy your credibility.

4. *Don't belittle anyone.*

If you mock anyone or use excessive sarcasm, it will usually backfire. If you try to communicate your message by ridiculing another person, members of the media will privately call you "a jerk," and you will not like the coverage you receive in the press.

One very important application of this rule is to never belittle your host on a radio or television talk show. I believe I faced the ultimate temptation in this regard. I once appeared on the *Donahue* show dealing with the Tennessee textbook case, which we discussed in Chapter 4. One of the issues raised was that the books were blatant in conveying a feminist ideology to little girls.

Phil Donahue stood about three feet away and said to me, "Well, Mike, the reason it's important that little girls learn this philosophy is so that they can stand on their own two feet in case they are abandoned by their husband later in life." A "zinger" comeback instantly popped into my head. I thought, but did not say, *You mean the way you left your first wife, Phil?*

True, I would have been known as the man who "zinged" Phil Donahue—but the Lord allowed me to see how much greater a victory it was for me to hold my tongue and avoid such belittling remarks.

One reward of holding my tongue was that I had another case that I felt deserved public attention, and I called Donahue's producer. They decided to do the show, and had me back again. In this way, I had a second opportunity to speak about Christian principles, simply because I was civil to the host under fire.

Even more important, I met a man in San Diego who recognized me from the *Donahue* show. He was a Christian, married to an unbeliever. His wife watched that show and told her husband that she was so impressed with the way the Christians handled themselves in front of a hostile audience that she was willing to go to church with him and begin thinking about his religious faith. If I had insulted Phil Donahue, that woman would not have responded favorably to Christianity. One "zing" may have cost one soul.

5. *Treat reporters as people.*

If you're dealing with an issue of any importance, you'll probably have more than one occasion to talk with the media. And if you are the kind of person drawn to these kinds of issues, you may have several occasions to talk with the same reporter. Treat the reporter as a guest, with decency and politeness.

At one point in my career I left Spokane and moved to Olympia to be able to lobby the Washington State legislature.

A reporter from the Spokane papers was located for a few months in Olympia with his family. We saw them at a shopping mall one night and invited them over for dinner with our family. We were both recent transplants with families who were missing their friends back in Spokane. It was a good evening for both families.

Although that reporter never slanted a story in my favor, he treated me fairly. I could always call him, and he would at least consider my side of a story he was reporting. At that time, I was involved in many controversial issues, and it would have been possible for the media to paint me as a "kook." But by treating reporters as people, with basic decency and civility, I was usually given a fair shake in the press.

If you build a relationship with members of the press as a truthful, straightforward, decent person you will be surprised at how much of the "left-wing bias" will disappear.

Now let's focus on some special types of media communications.

Letters to the Editor

A concise, well-reasoned letter to the editor is worth its weight in gold. I remember one example from when I was in college. Our city was debating the idea of buying some London double-decker buses to promote tourism and downtown shopping. There had been many articles written, much public debate in the city council, and many letters to the editor. Finally, one man wrote a letter that simply said, "London buses load on the left. Unless we want to run over the tourists, we need buses that load on the right." That short letter closed the entire debate.

Politicians regularly read letters to the editor. Such letters are very influential in conveying a message to elected officials.

The public reads these letters. You can get your views across to many more people than you could ever speak to by taking the time to write a good letter.

You will increase your chances of getting published if you:

Write well. Have someone check your spelling and grammar.

Learn to be concise. One page is maximum.

Make it interesting. Do not write a boring letter.

Write in a timely fashion. If something is being debated, write immediately.

Write sparingly. Every newspaper has a collection of "nuts" who write about every issue that comes along. Five letters per year is a reasonable limit.

Newspaper Reporters

Smaller, local newspapers are usually willing to print any kind of interesting story. Even the major daily newspapers will often report stories if you present them in a timely and informative manner.

If you are trying to generate coverage:

Make a reasonable assessment of whether or not your story is newsworthy. Not every dispute is worth printing in the paper. Do not have an inflated opinion of your own importance. One consequence of calling for press coverage on an issue that is really not that important is the same lesson learned by the boy who cried wolf. Someday you may really need press coverage and you will have been branded as a publicity hound who doesn't deserve coverage.

Write a one-to-two-page press release, giving appropriate facts and short quotations. Smaller papers may print this without a further interview. Larger papers will use this to determine whether or not your story is newsworthy.

Be sensitive to the newspaper's schedule. Reporters for morning newspapers generally work in the afternoon and evening. The best time to talk with such reporters is in the early to midafternoon. For afternoon papers, call first thing in the morning. If you allow them to scoop their morning rivals, you can be a long way toward getting good press coverage. And once the afternoon paper prints the story, it is almost obligatory for the morning paper to say something the following day. Stories for the Sunday paper are usually generated on Friday before noon.

If you are responding to a reporter:

Answer questions concisely. You can spend hours talking with a reporter and end up with twelve words in print. Conserve your time and theirs by learning to speak concisely.

Don't duck hard questions. Reporters will lose respect for you if you try to get out of answering hard questions. Answer the questions that are favorable to you as well as those unfavorable to you. You should anticipate all the hard questions you can be asked and be ready to give answers that you have previously thought through.

Don't put the reporter off for later. News is a very time-sensitive business. Rarely will a citizen get two chances to talk with a reporter. Promptly respond to any press inquiry.

Radio and Television Reporters

There are some additional suggestions that will help you get your message across in the broadcast media:

Learn to talk in "sound bites." You will be given about 10–15 seconds of airtime at the very most for most questions. Learn to say your essential information in one short segment. If a reporter asks you, "Why did you sue the school district over the sex-education program?" here are examples of a good sound bite and a bad sound bite.

Good answer:

"We've sued the school district because the Family Life Education program is forcing our children to become sexually experienced rather than teaching the simple facts of biology."

Bad answer:

"We don't like the Family Life Education program because we think it is too sexually explicit. They have far too much material about contraception and there is no good material on abstinence in the program. Kindergarten students are even included in sexually explicit education. We think the district has gone just too far. That's why we have hired a lawyer and filed this suit in the county court to back up our rights as parents to protect our children from this kind of material."

I can say the first answer in about 9 seconds. The second answer takes about 25 seconds. In most circumstances, you are going to be better off with the shorter answer. Otherwise, you will find that the reporter will take about 10 seconds out of your long answer and play it on the news.

Look nice when you are on television. Wear what you would wear to church or to a business function. Have a pleasant look on your face. It doesn't hurt to smile when appropriate. You should never scowl.

Use colorful language. If you can think of a good phrase that is short and colorfully explains your views, it is much more likely to get on the air than a bland statement.

Radio and Television Talk Shows

I like to do radio and television talk shows. I love doing a talk show where I am outnumbered by liberals. I especially love being outnumbered by liberal guests when the host is also a liberal. Why? Because America likes underdogs. If you go onto a show where the liberal producers have loaded the odds against you, rejoice because your job is to convince the audience—not the other guests. Since they have made you the underdog by sheer numbers, you will instantly have audience sympathy for you and consequently for your message.

While on television, you will look best if you dress well and learn correct television posture. Never sit back on a couch or soft chair. Sit on the edge of your seat with your back straight. If you lounge back you will look very silly on television.

Be aggressive on these shows, but not obnoxious. Do not wait to be asked a question every time. If you have a point you think is important, learn to speak quickly on the heels of someone else before the host turns to another matter.

Treat everyone with dignity. If you are being fired at, do not retaliate personally. Fire at their ideas and issues, but never fire at another person.

When you talk, do it with enthusiasm. Boring guests do not make good radio and television. You won't be asked back if you drone on and on.

America is heavily influenced by the media. One significant reason that the media appears to be tilted toward the left is that the left has learned to work with this medium better than conservatives. President Reagan was very conservative, but he was a master communicator and the media could not stop him from reaching the hearts of the American public. You can reach your fellow citizens with your message if you are concise, knowledgeable, interesting, and straightforward.

◊ **16** ◊

How to Be a Wise Litigant

Christians should be the last people to utter the words, "I'll see you in court." That kind of statement is the most overused threat in modern America. But there are times when we need to take our case to court to preserve our rights and to preserve America's freedoms.

A decision to take your case to court is an extremely important one, not to be made hastily. There are substantial costs of money and time. There are also emotional costs—it is very difficult to refrain from feeling combative or under attack. And your friends may not understand your dilemma. A decision to commence a lawsuit should be made with sanctified common sense, not as an emotional response to an injustice. Although there are costs, you should not avoid this course simply because it seems like too much of a hassle. Anything worth fighting for—and our liberties are certainly worth fighting for—will involve some turmoil and perhaps even some grief.

You should consider entering a lawsuit only as a last resort, when all other efforts to rectify a problem have failed.

Home School Legal Defense Association represents 24,000 home-schooling families. We could file 100 lawsuits a month if we wanted to litigate the rights of home-schooling parents. There would be several consequences if we did this. First, we would throw dozens of families every month into a world of unnecessary turmoil. "Trials and tribulations" is a scriptural phrase that accurately describes the emotions one can face when going through litigation. Second, we would lose more cases in litigation than we win in negotiation. Generally speaking, school administrators are more likely to understand what is going on and be reasonable than a judge who has no background in the area of home education. Third, there is no way we could afford to fight every battle faced by home schoolers in the expensive forum of the courtroom.

If we have a dispute over a requirement that children be tested in the public schools rather than in their homes, we are much better off if we can get a new law passed. If we win a lawsuit, more often than not we have solved the problem for only one family. If we get a law passed, we have solved the problem for everyone. The experience we have had in negotiating problems and finding political solutions for home schoolers is a lesson that I believe is generally applicable to other areas of concern.

If there are no other reasonable courses of action available, then you *begin* to consider litigation. Although at times this may be a bad decision, often seeking help from the courts is the very best thing you can do for yourself, your family, your church, or your country. We are going to consider some questions you should ask yourself to help decide when to go to court.

Before we look at these questions, I want to emphasize: *The Bible teaches that Christians should not sue other Christians.* No matter how meritorious your case may be, nothing merits violating Scripture.[1]

Guidelines for Evaluating Litigation

Here are some important factors to consider when you begin to think that a lawsuit may be necessary to preserve your freedoms or correct an injustice.

As you look at each question, you will notice that there

---

[1]This does not mean that Christians should not seek resolution of their legal disputes. As in any dispute between believers, the steps set forth in Matthew 18:15–17 need to be followed. If Christians are unable to resolve disputes between themselves in informal mediation, then I highly recommend that they seek the services of Christian Legal Society's Christian Conciliation Services. Disputes between Christians need to be resolved, and CLS offers a way to do this consistent with Scripture. (See Appendix for an address for CLS.)

is a lot of negative information, and this might discourage you from ever considering a lawsuit. I give you the facts only to give a realistic assessment of what's involved. In the second section, we'll consider the positive side of all these difficulties, which, under the right circumstances, more than compensate for the difficulties.

1. *Can you afford litigation?*

Lawsuits cost a lot of money and you need to have some way to pay the costs of a case you are planning to undertake. You either have to have the money yourself, be able to raise the money locally, or find a Christian legal organization that will take your case, and in that event they will raise the necessary funds.

Do not even think about starting a case with the hope that you can raise the money as you go along. If you do not have the money yourself, you should either get a Christian legal organization to take your case or raise virtually all of the necessary money locally before ever starting the case. Any lawyer worth having on your case will be experienced enough to know that "after-the-fact" fund-raising does not work. Raise the funds in advance.

Let me address one plague that pervades the Christian community. The "Christian freebie" plagues Christian doctors, dentists, counselors, as well as Christian lawyers. Many Christians believe that if they have a lawsuit, especially one involving religious freedom principles, any Christian lawyer in America should take on their case for free. Most cases involving issues of major importance require an enormous amount of time. The Betty Batey case we discussed in Chapter 6 took over nine weeks in trial, plus hundreds of hours of deposition and other pretrial hearings, as well as research and preparation. The Tennessee textbook trial took over 2,000 hours of lawyer time. A Christian lawyer might be able attend a school-board meeting at no charge, or go with you to a city council meeting for free. But when it comes to the courtroom, it is presumptuous to expect that a lawyer would devote hundreds or thousands of hours to your case for free. Would you work on your job for a quarter of the year for free?

Christian lawyers cannot afford to do that either.

If you approach a lawyer, do so on the assumption that you will be a paying client. If he volunteers to do the case for free, consider it a blessing.

There are three categories of legal expenses that must be evaluated: costs, attorney's fees, and the costs that can be awarded to the other side if you lose.

Basic costs. It costs an average of $100 to file a lawsuit in court. Pretrial depositions cost $200 to $500 each for the written transcript. If the lawyer has to travel to the deposition, there are travel expenses on top of that. If the witness is an expert in a given field such as medicine, education, engineering, or education, it may cost from $500 to $5,000 to pay the person for his time.

An average figure for costs in a religious liberties case would be around $10,000. These are the out-of-pocket expenses that must be paid or the case cannot progress.

Attorney's fees. There are two ways lawyers get paid: by the hour or on a contingency fee basis. The concept of paying a lawyer by the hour is easy to understand. Contingency fees are used in cases where the lawyer believes that the case is likely to win and there is a chance of a large cash payout at the end of the case. People who are injured in car wrecks or by medical malpractice can readily find a lawyer who will take their case on a contingency fee basis. At the end of the case the lawyer will usually get one-third of all the money involved. Lawyers who do this kind of work are gambling that most of the cases they take will return some money. If they lose, they get nothing. They must be skilled in evaluating these cases to be able to select those most likely to win. Most lawyers who specialize in these kinds of cases will make an initial evaluation of your case for free. It is well worth a consultation if you believe you have a case that might fit into these categories.

In most cases, the courts will not award *attorney's fees* to the winner that must be paid by the loser. There is an important exception that is relevant for most religious freedom cases. The courts will award attorney's fees to people who successfully sue the government or government officials for violating their civil rights. The only realistic way for an attorney to take a Christian-cause kind of case with no expectation of being paid an hourly rate by the client is if he believes that he can successfully win the civil rights case and be paid by the opponent. Religious freedom cases usually do not produce large enough money judgments to allow a lawyer to take these cases on a contingency fee basis.

Now having given you a sufficient dose of reality about legal costs, let me share with you how you can get your case litigated if you really do not have the money to spend but still believe it is necessary to fight for the principles we have talked about in this book.

A growing number of Christian organizations may take your case, and do it essentially for free. Obviously, there are substantial limitations on this offer. Most of these organizations work on a donation basis. In essence, they ask thousands of their members to each contribute money for your case. This is the way in which the cases I took for Concerned Women for America were financed. I was a staff attorney on a fixed salary. All of the costs for a case and all of my time plus the other salaries of those assisting me were paid by the generosity of CWA's faithful members.

Only a limited amount of money can be raised in this way and therefore only a limited number of cases can be undertaken by an organization. (In the Appendix you will find a list of legal organizations that take cases for free, and a brief summary of the kind of cases they look for. I have included in this list only those organizations willing to be listed.) These legal organizations can take only very selected cases they consider to be the best to advance some important legal principle in which they believe and are experienced. When I headed CWA's legal department, we turned down dozens of cases each month and took around five or six cases each year. Though many had merit, we had to be selective in order to win the cases that could benefit the greatest number of people.

Home School Legal Defense Association is unique in the way we fund our cases in court. We charge a membership fee up front of $100 per family per year. By having nearly 25,000-

member families, we are able to finance all of the thousands of legal conflicts and dozens of cases we encounter each year. We have a strict policy of not soliciting any funds through any mechanism. We are also unique in the fact that we guarantee every member that we will take their case as far as necessary for no charge beyond their membership fee.

Several Christian organizations are looking at our funding policies. I sincerely hope that groups which can guarantee the defense of Christian teachers, crisis pregnancy centers, and churches will come to fruition in the near future. The key to such groups will be the willingness of Christians to join the organization.

Costs that can be awarded to the other side if you lose. Generally, you do not face the prospect of having to pay the other side's attorney's fees even if you lose. The exception to this rule is if you file a frivolous lawsuit, you can be required to pay all of the costs the other side incurs. Normally, you will simply be required to pay the other side's out-of-pocket costs, which will be around the same amount of money you paid for your own costs—usually around $10,000.

In all my cases, there have been less than five where my clients have had to pay the other side's costs and no cases in which they have had to pay their opponents' attorney's fees. Usually, if a Christian organization has taken your case, they will stand in the gap for the costs that may be awarded to the other side.

2. *Where do you find a lawyer?*

Unless a Christian organization has taken your case (and they choose the lawyer), you will have to find a lawyer who will take your case. You really need to concentrate on finding someone with appropriate experience. A corporation would be absolutely foolish to ask me to review a question about securities or taxes. You would be foolish to ask a lawyer with exclusively corporate law experience to look at your case involving parental rights, religious freedom, or employment discrimination.

Christian Legal Society maintains a large list of lawyers who profess faith in Jesus Christ. You should be aware that there is a wide variety of religious backgrounds of the lawyers involved. Not all fit the mold that evangelical Christians would expect.

I regularly hire lawyers from other states to assist me in litigation in those states where I am not licensed. My first choice is to find an experienced Christian lawyer. If I cannot find such a person, I hire an experienced lawyer, rather than a Christian with no experience.

3. *Will your case set a bad precedent?*

Generally speaking, you should not file a lawsuit if you don't have a good chance of winning. Litigation is too expensive to do it just to make a point. If you merely want to make a point, get yourself invited to be on a radio talk show.

I am more willing than many to take a case that appears to be an uphill fight. We are facing a judicial system that is not very friendly to Christian values. Most cases that Christians care about are litigated against the government, and it is very difficult to win a case—any case—against the government. I recently won a case in the South Carolina Supreme Court against the State Department of Education. I was told that this was only the second case that the department had ever lost.

If a wise and experienced lawyer tells you that your case is likely to lose and it will also set a bad precedent for other people facing similar situations, listen to his counsel.

4. *Can you stand up under the pressure?*

Vicki Frost underwent tremendous abuse and criticism from those in her community when she stood against the humanistic textbooks forced on her children. The other parents in that case also experienced attack, but Vicki was the leader and she got the abuse in multiplied measure. The seven fathers who stood up for freedom in Nebraska spent ninety-three days in jail, many lost their jobs, some lost their homes, and their wives and children had to flee the state. The pain and agony Betty Batey went through in her case is something that not one of us would ever desire.

These are the three cases that exerted the most extreme

pressure on my clients. But every case I have ever been involved in had at least some pressure on the people. If you have not learned to rely on God in times of trouble, a lawsuit is not for you.

Let me be quick to point out that God has proven himself to be strong in the lives of my clients. He has been sufficient in some extraordinary circumstances, even in the three cases I have identified as being the most trying.

5. *What if you are sued?*

Many of the cases we have considered have been ones in which I have represented the plaintiffs, that is, the people who started the lawsuit. And our discussion so far has considered only the possibility that you would want to sue someone for violating your rights or values. We need to recognize that you may find yourself needing a lawyer because you, your church, or your organization has been sued. It has been my observation that it is easier to find a Christian organization willing to defend you if you are being sued than it is to find one to initiate a lawsuit at your request. It is also easier to find a local Christian lawyer willing to take the case for free or reduced rates.

Being easier does not mean it is guaranteed. You may end up spending a lot of money for your own defense. (Consider the possibility that your homeowner's insurance may cover the costs of some kinds of cases.) Therefore, it's wise whenever possible to follow our Lord's admonition to make peace with your enemy when he drags you off to court.

A Reason for Encouragement

If you have worked your way through the tough process outlined in this chapter, and you still find yourself in a position where you are able and willing to continue, you can feel confident that this course of action is probably God's will. (This statement assumes that the other *indicia* of God's will for your life have also been considered. These include leading from Scripture, prompting from the Holy Spirit, concurrence of opinion between husband and wife, and advice from pastor and elders.)

Litigation is never fun, but the results are often joyous. I have had the pleasure of seeing Betty Batey's face when the trial judge dismissed all criminal charges against her. The day the seven fathers were released from jail in Nebraska was like all the first days of spring all of them had experienced in their entire lives. When the Supreme Court of South Carolina informed me of our recent victory, the party we had over the phone with our faithful leaders in that state was more than a little exuberant.

Personal victories are very satisfying. Victories when you have battled for godly principles are absolutely exhilarating. The system of American justice does not always work well for Christians. When it does, the joy of having stood for righteousness and having established a principle of law that will help many other people makes all the work, expense, and turmoil seem a small price to have paid.

In the last chapter, we will see how God often grants ultimate justice to those who have been denied justice in the courts of man. But first, I want to talk about the power and impact that comes when a church decides to take a stand.

Stand Up Without Losing Balance

In the battle for the future of America, Christians have a significant organizational advantage. While humanists have substantial influence over the schools and media, Christians meet together once a week at church, and this provides a far more effective means of organizing people for action.

There is much that can be accomplished through church organizational structure. Alerts can be issued urging people to write on state or federal legislation. Announcements can be made to get people to a school-board meeting. Collections can be taken to help pay for the legal defense of a case. Prayer needs can be shared for Christians suffering persecution in a foreign country.

I have found, however, that there is a lot of resistance to bringing issues and actions of this kind into churches. Many pastors have justifiable concerns that cause them to hesitate. In other churches the pastor is willing to lead in this way, but the elders resist for reasons of their own.

Two issues are consistently raised, and they clearly fall into the category of "justifiable concerns." First, many churches want to avoid the trap of the "social gospel"—that is, viewing social improvement as a means to bring salvation. Second, Christian leaders are concerned that people will become over committed to social issues at the expense of other priorities of the church, such as evangelism, missions, and discipleship. Let's deal with each of these concerns in turn.

The Two Biggest Concerns

"Social gospel." This term was invented to describe a theological movement that overtook a number of Protestant denominations in the early part of this century. The advocates of this movement urged churches to act in order to alleviate the social problems of the day, with a special concern for poverty. There is nothing wrong with such efforts in and of themselves. The problem that developed was that those most insistent on social action tended to be the ones who denied the infallibility of Scripture. Their low view of Scripture led to a denial of the supernatural, which in turn led to a denial of the deity of Christ. Believing that Christ was only a "good man," the good news of the gospel was changed from a means to save man from his individual sin into a means to save mankind from the evils of society.

The advocates of the "social gospel" erred because they saw social action as a substitute for the real gospel. Anyone who turns his back on man's primary need for personal salvation through Jesus Christ as the only solution for man's sin problem has fallen away from the core of the Christian faith and is preaching "a different gospel." The apostle Paul warned us that there is no "good news" in a gospel that substitutes man's works for Christ's sacrifice (Galatians 1:6–7).

The only reason that the advocates of the social gospel were successful in seducing many Christian denominations to their way of thinking is that they took a truth from Scripture—the need to help our society—and perverted this secondary truth by substituting it for the primary truth of Scripture.

Christians have many duties that are clear from Scripture. We have responsibilities that stem from every relationship in life. All have the responsibility to serve and love God. All husbands have the responsibility to love their wives. Wives have the duty to be a loving and submissive aid to their husbands. Parents are to train up their children in the nurture and admonition of the Lord. Children are to obey their parents. Employers are to treat their employees fairly. Employees are to be productive and obedient workers. Citizens are to obey the laws of the nation and are called on to stand up for righteousness and the principles of God in the conduct of the affairs of the nation (Psalm 94:16; Proverbs 14:34).

As a Christian husband, I recognize that I have a duty to love my wife. But loving my wife is no substitute for preaching the gospel just as preaching the gospel is no substitute for loving my wife. In the same way, while there has been error in substituting social action for the real gospel, it would be another error to ignore the biblical mandate to follow the principles of God in relation to our duties as citizens.

Wrong priorities. I would not want to be a part of a church where abortion issues, religious freedom concerns, and the legal rights of the family became predominant issues Sunday after Sunday. As important as these issues are, they are only secondary issues in terms of the whole mission of the church. These and the other issues we have discussed in this book should not be ignored in churches, but they should never be allowed to dominate the life of a church.

This is not to say that individual Christians within the church cannot have this "citizenship responsibility" as their individual area of primary ministry. In fact, I hope that every church would have people whose primary area of ministry would be in the arena of Christian citizenship. And I hope that they would be encouraged, supported and given some platform to speak and rally support. This is an application of the truth of Scripture that God gifts people in many different ways (1 Corinthians 12). Some are the hands, some the feet, and some the eyes in the body of Christ. Some are called to youth ministry, some to help the singles, some to use sports as a means to conduct evangelism, and some to assist in the area of Christian citizenship. To maintain individual balance, it must also be remembered that even though we may be called to a primary area of ministry, this does not mean that this is our exclusive duty as a Christian.

Frankly, there are two problems I've seen with Christian citizen "activists" in churches. One is that they tend to look down on other people in the church who are not as active on these issues as they are. Conversely, I see people who are called to other spheres of ministry, such as missions, who also look down on those who are not as committed to their special area of concern. Brothers and sisters, let's stop the tug-of-war: *People are called individually by God.* A well-rounded local church will have people who are serving in many different areas with a real appreciation for those who are called to minister in spheres different than their own. God want us to be a voice of salvation and of justice.

The ideal plan for an "active" church. In my judgment, as an elder and an experienced activist, the best way for a church to be involved and balanced is to execute a plan something like the following. A committee should be created called the Christian Citizenship Committee. It should fit in with the overall church governance just like a Christian Education Committee. Depending on the size of the church, from five to a dozen people should serve on this committee.

The overall duties of this committee would be to:

- Research issues of potential concern such as abortion, pornography and other matters of public morality, religious freedom, Christian schools, home schools, and other local and national issues;
- Alert church leadership and the church body when steps of action are necessary;
- Provide information for appropriate subjects of prayer for our nation, state, and community, especially prayer for the leaders of our nation.

Leading the Way

Recently, I attended a prayer breakfast sponsored by a church on the other side of the county in which I live. The purpose of the breakfast was to honor and welcome the new members of the County Board of Supervisors. Seven of the nine members of the board showed up to mingle with pastors and Christian laity from a number of churches. Every one of the elected officials said that they genuinely appreciated the honor of the meeting, and asked if the church would sponsor such breakfasts three or four times a year so that they would not lose touch with the people of the county.

By simply hosting a breakfast, one church's Christian Citizenship Committee could insure that your local officials received regular input from Christians. You can be sure that there will be political benefits from such gatherings. The world of politics is a world of relationships and issues. Your church could be drawn into a zoning issue, or some neighbors could complain that your church is a cult practicing a strange religion that should be kept out of the county. If members of the Board of Supervisors have a personal relationship with members of your church, they are not likely to believe false allegations. And you have the chance to encourage your elected officials to pursue righteous laws with a proper respect for the rights of minorities and the principles of religious freedom.

At least one member of your Christian Citizenship Committee should get on the mailing list of every major Christian organization dealing with these areas of concern. You should make sure that you are in league with both state and local organizations as well as the national organizations. Also it would be good to have members of the committee regularly monitor Christian news sources such as *World* magazine, radio news from *Family News in Focus* and *USA Radio News,* and the Christian talk programs such as *Point of View* with Marlin Maddoux and, of course, *Focus on the Family,* which often addresses issues calling for action.

The Christian Citizenship Committee could produce a bulletin insert approximately once a month, giving a briefing on issues of concern. Any special calls to action that have been approved by church leadership should appear in the bulletin, emphasized by a special announcement from the pulpit.

If the law in your state permits this, once a year this committee should arrange for voting registrars to come to your church to register people to vote after a Sunday morning service. The committee could also distribute the kind of candidate surveys described in Chapter 13. It is very important to remember that the tax laws absolutely prohibit churches from endorsing or opposing candidates. The committee can pass out objective information stating candidates' positions, but it must not expressly or implicitly endorse one candidate over another.

One church I know regularly sponsors candidate forums for those running for local office. They run their meetings much along the lines established by the League of Women Voters. All candidates from all parties are invited. Each is given an allotment of time and then the audience is allowed to ask questions. People from other churches in the community are encouraged to attend. The church is not obligated to endorse anyone after such a forum. The people find it easy to decide once they hear the candidates for themselves.

What Role Will We Play?

If the majority of Bible-believing churches in this country were organized for this kind of Christian citizenship activity, our points of view would play a major role in every decision that is made on matters of significance to our people. We have so much to gain by taking this kind of action. We have nothing to lose, provided we keep this ministry in balance with the whole counsel of God, and understand that the first priority of every church is to preach the gospel of Jesus Christ.

◇ **18** ◇

God's Final Chapters

American Christians seem to expect that we are going to win every skirmish and every battle. In reality, there are times when we will lose. Sometimes we lose cases in court. Sometimes our petitions to the city council fall on deaf ears. Often Congress just doesn't want to do the right thing.

From personal experience, I can say losing does not feel good. But one of the first things that most Christians learn is that Jesus is Lord of our feelings. In other words, our God specializes in ministering to those who appear to have lost everything from the world's perspective. He is sufficient to meet our needs when our feelings tell us that we have "lost" everything.

We must recognize that sometimes we are going to face injustices. We live in an imperfect world with people who still possess a fallen nature. Some injustices will only be remedied in heaven. But I've been at this business long enough now to see some injustices set right here on earth. It does take a while, but the hand of God is unmistakable. When the United States Supreme Court says "appeal denied, case closed," God sometimes gives us evidence that they are not really the highest court of all.

The Father of All Fathers

I've mentioned several times the case of the fathers from Nebraska who were jailed for ninety-three days. When they were released it was a day of great joy, but that joy was mixed with apprehension because the law which had regulated Christian schools in an excessive manner was still on the books. And this law had been tested all the way to the U.S. Supreme Court and was upheld when the high court refused to hear the appeal.

The chief in-court adversary had been the attorney general of Nebraska. He continued to claim that this law was still valid and he would uphold it.

But the governor of Nebraska, Bob Kerrey, appointed a study committee to see if there was a solution to this problem that had plagued not just this one school but numerous Christian schools in the state. The chairman of the committee was the past president of the Nebraska Bar Association. There was a professor of constitutional law appointed as well as a retired educator and other business and community leaders. The composition of the committee did not seem to lend itself to a favorable result.

To our amazement the result was favorable indeed! The committee determined that there had been serious constitutional violations under the old law, and they recommended that it be repealed and replaced. That is exactly what happened. The new law granted appropriate freedom to Christian schools and home schools, and Nebraska has been virtually free of these problems since that time.

In the meantime, the attorney general who had been the Christian schools' most vigorous opponent found himself involved in an unrelated financial scandal. Just when the Christian schools saw this new law coming forward with promise, they saw their archenemy being ridden out of town on a rail. A new attorney general was appointed by Governor Kerrey. His selection? Although this man was a Republican and Kerrey a Democrat, he appointed the man who had chaired the study committee. He had done such a good job resolving a persistent difficulty, the governor knew he was the man to fill the vacancy.

And while all this was happening, the Eighth Circuit Court of Appeals held that the action of the Cass County sheriff in raiding the church worship service in connection with this entire dispute was a violation of the worshipers' civil rights and awarded us over $45,000 in attorney's fees. The attorney general's office had to write us the check to pay the bill.

Fathers had been imprisoned, schools had been closed, raids of churches had been conducted, and yet we seemed to lose every round. Finally, though, it all started to turn and justice was obtained through a new law and a favorable court decision. It took a long time, but God, the Father of these Christian dads, clearly wrote the final chapter.

A Surprise in the Iowa Senate

Final chapters come in every context. Iowa was one of the last three states to cling to an old-style anti-home school law that required parents to be certified teachers. Several court challenges had failed. There was no success in the legislative process to replace this law with a more favorable home-schooling statute.

The legal and political climates were so bad that the only law which appeared to have a chance for success was a bill introduced to make the situation even worse. The enemies of home education decided to move home-school prosecutions from criminal court to juvenile court. On the surface this sounded like a small improvement, but in reality it would be a huge setback. In criminal court, people have some rights that cannot be readily violated. In juvenile court, the parents would now be prosecuted for a version of child abuse (in Iowa they call it CHINA, which stands for Child In Need of Assistance). Instead of paying fines or facing jail, parents now faced losing custody of their children. Home schoolers did everything they knew to do, but politically they seemed to be getting nowhere.

In the 1989 session of the Iowa legislature, the CHINA bill passed both houses of the legislature, but in slightly different forms. Until a bill passes both houses in identical format and then is signed by the governor, it doesn't become law.

So the bill came back for the continuing session in 1990. These two versions of the CHINA bill were deadlocked. Finally, however, a compromise agreement was reached between the leaders of both houses. The new version of the CHINA bill quickly passed through the Iowa House of Representatives. But the battle in the Senate was closer.

Home-school leaders took a pre-vote count. It appeared that there were 26 votes for the CHINA bill and 24 votes against it. Because of the procedural posture of the bill, 26 votes were required as the minimum vote for passage.

Home schoolers prayed for God's intervention. And when the day of the vote came, they thought they had seen an answer. While the debate was going on, one senator came out into the lobby and asked to speak with the home-schooling leaders. He told them—take note of this—that he was having trouble sleeping because this issue was bothering him. He asked if there was a home-schooling family in his district he could talk to. A call was immediately arranged to a family in his district. He went back onto the floor of the Senate and made a speech in favor of parents' rights and announced his opposition to the CHINA bill.

The home schoolers were ecstatic since they now had a 25–25 split. Their opponents couldn't get 26 votes. Or so they thought. Someone pointed out that in case of tie, the lieutenant governor cast the tie-breaking vote. He would supply the 26th vote and was a sworn opponent of the home schoolers. Spirits sank again when this information was shared.

The vote came. There were 25 for the CHINA bill and, surprisingly, 24 against the bill. One of the home schoolers most staunch allies was absent. He simply "lost track" of the time while at another engagement. Our opponents kept the vote open for over 45 minutes—a record. They wanted the missing senator to show up, knowing that his vote would cause a tie. If they could get their tie, then the lieutenant governor could supply the 26th vote in their favor.

It was a very unusual situation—if we had gotten one more favorable vote, we would have lost. None of the home schoolers could have planned this outcome. It was simply too unexpected and too complex. I believe that we won because God blinded the eyes of one of the friends of home schooling to the correct time.

This episode caused such a radical shift in political momentum that in 1991, the legislature passed a new, far more lenient law on home schooling.

Betty Batey's Patient Victory

No episode in my career has taught me the importance of waiting on God's final chapter more than the case of Betty Batey, who was fighting for her own freedom and for custody of her son, Brian.

You will recall that Brian had been placed in a Christian foster home at the end of the trial between Betty, a Pentecostal Christian, and Frank, her homosexual ex-husband. But the court also required Brian to get psychological counseling. For an extended time Brian kept telling the psychologist that he wanted to live with his mother. As long as he said that he was considered by both the court and the psychologist to be too immature to be allowed to make his own decisions.

Through some of his own actions, Brian ended up in a series of foster homes. And finally, he caught on to the system. If he continued to ask to live with his mother, he would remain in foster care. If he asked to live with his father, he would be set free. So that's what he did, and he was sent to live with his father in Palm Springs.

That was very hard for Betty. Although I had left Concerned Women for America and was no longer personally handling the case, I stayed in touch with her. While it was very difficult for her to handle, she always told me that she had faith that God was going to eventually return Brian to her. And she had faith that God was going to bring Brian back to himself, for it was apparent that he was slipping—not in the ways of homosexuality, but in other areas of worldly living that were permitted by his father.

Then came the most unexpected twist of all: Frank Batey died of AIDS. When he took the witness stand for my cross-examination in Betty's second trial for kidnapping, he looked gaunt and weak. He denied having AIDS, but he proved to have concealed the truth to the end. Just a few weeks later he was dead.

The unexpected and hurtful twist came when Brian chose to remain living in Palm Springs with Frank's ex-lover. Brian went to court and asked for the court to officially sanction this placement. There was no suggestion of homosexuality.

Brian simply wanted to live in the atmosphere where he would not be subject to Christian moral restraints. Betty was deeply hurt when Brian made this request, but was wounded even more when the judge awarded custody to the ex-lover!

Since I was no longer the attorney for Betty, I called to see how she was doing. Her new lawyer, one of my former co-workers at CWA, assured me that Betty continued to believe that God was not through yet. And she was right.

Several months later, Brian voluntarily returned to his mother and walked the aisle at church, coming back to God. Betty and Brian left California and took up residence in another state for a season to have time and distance to heal old wounds and break old patterns.

No matter how badly the courts had treated her, Betty Batey had faith in the ultimate Judge of the Universe. He proved himself strong on her behalf, vindicating her years of faith in spite of the darkness that threatened to engulf her.

Conclusion

As we look toward the future of our nation and our freedoms, there are three kinds of reality we must consider.

Dark clouds on the horizon. First, as we look at the world about us we realize that there are times when we will face the darkness of dashed hopes and dreams, perhaps even the darkness of injustice and persecution. Common sense tells us that there may be dark days ahead for decent people in our land. The moral problems that took the forefront of Christian concerns in the early 1980s have not been diminished, but instead seem like an insatiable monster devouring our moral fiber with wanton callousness. Religious freedom is at an all-time low in the American Republic, while taxes and debt are both at all-time highs.

We are at a crossroads of our national history. America is increasingly in debt. Financially this is obvious. Our national debt threatens to make our children and grandchildren economic slaves. They will be paying with their lives and freedoms for the excesses of our present bureaucratic extravagance.

Our national moral debt is no less staggering. The AIDS crisis is just the down payment that is required for our years of reckless licentiousness. Abortion, divorce, and adultery also produce moral consequences that must be paid.

The reality of faith. Common sense is not the only way to look at problems. We need to look at problems through the eyes of faith and with the eyes of experience detailed in this book. We have seen repeated episodes where the actions of faithful people have produced results that defied the experts.

America has the three ingredients that are necessary for a future that shines in brightness. First, we have the heritage of our forefathers who taught us the principles of moral and political freedom based upon the precepts of God's Word. Second, we have the constitutional system of government that permits us to take wrongs and turn them into rights and take those officials who permit or cause wrongs and peacefully turn them into ex-officials. And, third, we have people with the kind of faith that takes action.

The only question is: *Do we have enough people with this kind of faith?* Each of us can take the kind of individual actions we have described in this book—standing for our rights and, more importantly, standing for what is right. And collectively, we can take action as well.

Our potential for a bright future can become a reality. There is a simple but profound solution to these two areas of national crisis—our financial and moral indebtedness. Good people must stand up. We must demand an end to the recklessness that has driven both our economic and moral policies. If good people stand up, cry out "enough is enough," and take action in accord with our beliefs, these dark clouds will burn off like a morning mist.

As we have seen with the seven fathers in Nebraska, the home schoolers in Iowa, and especially in the case of Betty Batey, God is ready to respond. He will write the last chapter for people who step out in faith.

It's up to us to take the first step, though. It's time to draw the line.

Appendix

NATIONAL ORGANIZATIONS

American Association of Christian Schools

National Office:
P.O. Box 2189
Independence, MO 64055
(816)795–7709

Washington, D.C. Office:
P.O. Box 1088
Fairfax, VA 22030
(703)818–7150

The American Association of Christian Schools has been providing consistent effective leadership both in state and national governments for over twenty years. The legislative purpose is:

1. To protect our schools and ministries from government entanglement;
2. To promote the causes of religious freedom, Christian education and family values;
3. To influence legislation that would help or hurt our cases;
4. To inform our legislators of our concerns and compliments; and
5. To challenge our nation to consider biblical answers for man's problems.

American Center for Law and Justice

Keith A. Fournier, Executive Director
P.O. Box 64429
Virginia Beach, VA 23467
804–523–7570
804–523–7546 FAX

The American Center for Law and Justice is a nonprofit public interest law firm founded by Dr. M. G. "Pat" Robertson in 1990. The center is unqualifiedly and unapologetically pro-liberty, pro-life, and pro-family. The center provides legal assistance in a broad range of areas, including religious freedom in schools, in the workplace and in the public square.

The American Center for Law and Justice has established the "Abortion Victims' Rights Project" in order to assist women who have been victimized by abortion-related medical malpractice. The project provides monies for nonlegal expenses of litigation, and works with private practitioners who are handling such malpractice cases.

The center publishes a journal entitled *Law and Justice* and has established an affiliated network of attorneys throughout the country committed to assisting in its public interest efforts.

American Family Association Law Center

Benjamin W. Bull, General Counsel
P.O. Drawer 2440
Tupelo, MS 38803
601–844–5036
601–844–9176 FAX

The American Family Association (AFA) Law Center is a nonprofit legal entity that defends and prosecutes the civil rights of Christians. It is an arm of the American Family Association, a pro-family ministry with over 600 local chapters and 450,000 members. The AFA Law Center provides legal assistance on issues related to abortion, pornography, school prayer, religious discrimination, free exercise of religion, freedom of expression, boycotts, picketing, and other matters having constitutional significance for Christians. It has five salaried staff attorneys and over 400 pro-bono volunteer attorneys across the country.

Association of Christian Schools International

731 N. Beach Boulevard
La Habra, CA 90631

P.O. Box 4097
Whittier, CA 90607–4097
213–694–4791
213–690–6234 FAX

The Association of Christian Schools International (ACSI) is the largest Christian school organization in the world, serving a combined membership of 530,000 students and 2,800 schools. ACSI is a full-service association that offers such services as teacher and administrator conventions, school accreditation, teacher certification and student activities. The association also publishes curriculum and materials for Christian educators.

Christian Action Council

Thomas A. Glessner, President
101 W. Broad Street, Suite 500
Falls Church, VA 22046–4200
703–237–2100
703–237–8276 FAX

The Christian Action Council (CAC), founded in 1975, exists to raise a biblical Christian voice in the councils of government and courts of law where biblical principles, human rights and civil and criminal laws intersect. Since its establishment, it has concerned itself primarily with issues relating to endangered human life, in abortion, fetal research, genetic engineering, assisted suicide, euthanasia, and the "right to die." The independently chartered Christian Action Council Education and Ministries Fund provides ministry and educational materials, training, and advice for alternatives to abortion, post-abortion counseling and related services to crisis pregnancy centers in the United States, Canada and other countries, over 400 of which are directly affiliated with CAC. The council's cooperation with the International Seminar is intended to equip concerned Christians with legal, biblical, and theological resources in order to foster intelligent and effective Christian participation in public policy discourse and formation, particularly in the area of the right to life.

Christian Advocates Serving Evangelism

Jay Sekulow, Chief Counsel
P.O. Box 450349
Atlanta, GA 30345
404–633–2444
404–634–3785 FAX

Christian Advocates Serving Evangelism is specifically dedicated to the ideal that religious freedom and freedom of speech are inalienable, God-given rights. The purpose of CASE is to educate, promulgate, conciliate and, where necessary, litigate to the end that Christians' rights are protected under the law.

CASE handles cases involving free speech in public areas such as parks, sidewalks, streets, and public transportation terminals. Contact Jay Sekulow, Chief Counsel. CASE also has begun a national campaign to see that public secondary school students are not denied their rights to meet together or distribute literature on their campuses. Contact Joe Thornton.

Christian Legal Society

Bradley P. Jacob, Executive Director
4208 Evergreen lane, Suite 222
Annandale, VA 22003
703–642–1070
703–642–1075 FAX

Christian Legal Society is a nationwide membership organization of Christian lawyers, judges, law professors and law students from all denominations and political persuasions. Founded in 1961, CLS's mission is to equip, inspire and challenge lawyers and law students to serve Jesus Christ effectively through the legal profession. This is done by means of publications, national and regional conferences, local chapters, Bible studies and discussion groups of lawyers and law students. As Christian attorneys develop a vision for Christian commitment in their professional lives, they are challenged to serve the church and the community through public outreach ministries, including Christian conciliation, legal aid services for the poor, and the Center for Law and Religious Freedom. Since 1975, the center has worked through its professional staff and volunteer attorneys across the United States to defend the fundamental, inalienable rights of all people, particularly the right of religious liberty. For more information, membership materials or referrals to Christian lawyers anywhere in the country, please contact CLS at the above address and telephone.

Christian Solidarity International-USA

Rev. Steven L. Snyder, President (USA)
Michael P. Farris, Chairman (USA)
P.O. Box 70563
Washington, DC 20024
301–989–0298
301–989–0398 FAX

Christian Solidarity International (CSI) is a nonsectarian, human rights, and humanitarian organization helping persecuted Christians worldwide. Headquartered in Switzerland and with offices worldwide, CSI gathers information on victims of oppression and helps by organizing prayer campaigns, mobilizing delegations, raising public awareness, and providing practical assistance. With religious freedoms increasingly under attack, CSI serves on an international level in the battle to preserve this fundamental axiom of all human rights.

Concerned Women for America

Beverly LaHaye, President
370 L'Enfant Promenade, S.W.
Suite 800
Washington, DC 20024
202–488–7000
202–488–0806 FAX

Founded in 1979 by Beverly LaHaye, Concerned Women for America (CWA) is the nation's largest grassroots women's organization that promotes Judeo-Christian and family values in law and public policy. CWA has local chapters in all fifty states and national legislative and legal headquarters in the nation's capital. CWA's Legal Department, created in 1983, handles many religious freedom and constitutional rights cases. CWA broadcasts *Beverly LaHaye Live,* a national daily radio show focusing on issues affecting the family, and publishes *Family Voice,* its monthly news magazine.

Equal Employment Opportunity Commission

1801 L Street, N.W.
Washington, DC 20036
General Information, 202–663–4264

Family Life Ministries

Dr. Timothy LaHaye
370 L'Enfant Promenade, S.W., Suite 801
Washington, DC 20024
202–488–0700

The purpose of Family Life Ministries is to minister to the family through Family Life Seminars and to educate the Christian community through television, radio, and printed materials.

The *Capital Report* is a monthly report on key issues in government that impact family, traditional moral values, and religious freedom. An introduction copy can be obtained by writing to the above address. A one-year subscription is available for a donation of $15.00 or more per year.

The *Education Report* is a monthly publication produced for Christian schools to alert their members and prospects on the real conditions in the public schools that jeopardize family moral and religious values. The reason more Christian parents don't send their children to a Christian school is that they don't really know what is going on in the public school. The *Education Report* informs them. This report is mailed to Christian schools, camera-ready, for their personalized printing and mailing as a publicity piece for $20.00 a month.

Family Research Council

Gary L. Bauer, President
700 Thirteenth Street, N.W., Suite 500
Washington, DC 20005
202–393–2100
202–393–2134

The Family Research Council is an independent, non-profit, advocacy organization dedicated to ensuring that the interests of the family are considered and respected in the formation of public policy. The council works to create in the legislative, executive and judicial branches of the federal government an understanding of the overall pro-family agenda. The council also maintains an extensive educational outreach that equips individuals nationwide to address family issues and activates these citizens to influence the legislative and public policy process. Founded in 1981, the Family Research Council merged with the Colorado-based Focus on the Family in October 1988, and operates as a division of one of the largest pro-family organizations in the nation. To accomplish its goals, the Family Research Council works in key areas to advocate a pro-family agenda. They are Government Relations, Research/Policy Development, Media, Coalition Building, Corporate and Community Outreach. The public can get involved in pro-family political activities through action items in *Washington Watch,* a monthly newsletter that focuses on current family issues in the nation's Capital; and stay informed with *Family Policy,* a bi-monthly publication containing in-depth analysis of major policy issues and trends. Constituents may write to or call Lorianne Merritt at the above address or telephone numbers.

Focus on the Family

102 N. Cascade
Colorado Springs, CO 80903
719–531–3400
719–473–9751 FAX

Free Congress Foundation & Coalitions for America

Paul M. Weyrich, President
717 Second Street, N.E.

Free Congress Foundation

Washington, DC 20002
202–546–3000
202–543–5605 FAX

The Free Congress Foundation is a 14-year-old nonprofit organization dedicated to the promotion of a public policy agenda that reflects traditional American values. The foundation bases its program activities on the established principles of Western culture and democratic capitalism. The foundation recognizes the importance of restoring those values and principles and continues to develop action-oriented programs designed to encourage American citizens to insist on serious consideration of traditional values in the creation of public policy. The foundation's Coalitions for America is the lobbying arm that works through the legislative process to integrate these traditional American values.

In addition to being a recognized leader in the movement to restore traditional values in the American political process, the foundation has led the way in teaching the principles and techniques of good governance to those countries in the process of adopting a democratic form of government. At both home and abroad, the Free Congress Foundation seeks to empower the individual citizen to understand and accept the responsibility of a "government by the people."

Home School Legal Defense Association

Michael P. Farris, Founder & President
P.O. Box 159
Hwy. 9 at Rt. 781
Paeonian Springs, VA 22129
703–882–3838
703–882–3628 FAX

Home School Legal Defense Association was founded in 1983 for the purpose of providing legal protection for families who have chosen to educate their children at home. HSLDA is a Christian organization with a Christian board of directors and staff. However, since its inception, HSLDA has held the position that its responsibility is to protect the interests of every home-schooling member family, no matter what their religious affiliation. The membership fee is $100 per year, per family, which provides full representation at every stage of legal proceedings at no cost for attorneys' fees beyond the annual fee. In 1990 the National Center for Home Education was created to track both federal and state legislation impacting families and education, as well as to provide resources for state home-schooling organizations.

National Legal Foundation

Robert K. Skolrood, Director
6477 College Park Square, Suite 306
Virginia Beach, VA 23464
804–424–4242
800–397–4242 Toll Free
804–420–0855 FAX

The National Legal Foundation is a public interest law firm dedicated to the preservation of Americans' God-given freedoms and constitutional rights. It actively defends citizens' freedoms of religion, speech and assembly. Among other significant accomplishments, the National Legal Foundation provided lead counsel in the case *Mergens* v. *Westside Community Schools,* in which the United States Supreme Court upheld the right of public high school students to form voluntary, on-campus Bible clubs. In addition to its effective advocacy, the National Legal Foundation recognizes a continuing duty to educate the public in a proper understanding of their inalienable rights.

Services: Legal representation, research, brief writing, referrals, educational materials.

Projects: Affiliate attorneys network; summer internship program; legal news bulletins by fax.

Publications: *The NLF Minuteman* (quarterly newsletter)
Minuteman Alert (monthly bulletin)
Occasional paper services
Broadcast: *The Minuteman Alert* radio program

The Rutherford Institute

John W. Whitehead, President
International Headquarters
P.O. Box 7482
1445 East Rio Road
Charlottesville, VA 22906–7482
804–978–3888
804–978–1789 FAX

The Rutherford Institute is a nonprofit, tax-exempt legal defense organization that provides free legal representation to those whose religious liberties are threatened. It consists of an international network of attorneys committed to aggressively defending the constitutional rights of religious people.

Western Center for Law & Religious Freedom

David L. Llewellyn, Jr., President & Special Counsel
Jack Hafer, Executive Director
1211 H Street, Suite A
Sacramento, CA 95814
916–447–4111
916–447–5191 FAX

Northwest Office:
Gregory Casey, Special Counsel

West 1402 Broadway Avenue
Spokane, WA 99201
509–325–5850
509–326–7503 FAX

The Western Center for Law and Religious Freedom is a public interest law firm that provides legal and educational services, without charge, to activist organizations, churches, concerned citizens and lawyers throughout the nation, particularly in the western states, to stand for "Liberty and Justice under God."

WCLRF defends the constitutional liberties and God-given inalienable rights upon which America is founded: right to life; religious and civil liberties; parent and family rights; standards in public education; and justice in public institutions.

WCLRF offers "Christian Citizenship Seminars" for churches and the Christian community, providing a free session of legal consultation to the church pastoral and administrative staff (including a review of current legal controversies relating to church ministries) and a seminar for parents, Christian activists, and members of the congregation.

WCLRF also offers "continuing legal education" courses for attorneys on various aspects of religious liberty.

RECOMMENDED PUBLICATIONS

Citizen Magazine

Citizen, published monthly by Focus on the Family, is a 16-page magazine filled with news updates and insightful analyses of issues impacting the families of America. Topics covered include divorce, abortion, pornography, the gay rights movement, the media, and politics. In addition, each issue lists practical steps that readers can take to make an impact in their communities.

Citizen is available for a donation of $20 for a one-year subscription or $35 for two years. Order by Visa or MasterCard by calling 1–800-A-FAMILY or write to Focus on the Family, Colorado Springs, CO 80995.

World Magazine

World is the only weekly news magazine of its kind. It provides the latest-breaking news, incisive news analysis, and thought-provoking commentary 40 times a year (biweekly during the summers and winter holidays). *World* is not a "how-to" publication. You won't be told what to do or how to think. But it is a quality news magazine that allows the reader to draw his own conclusions and take action. Each issue has national and international reporting, news on the life issues—from legislation in Washington and the states to developments in the law—and from the world of religion, and a regenerate look at the often unregenerate world of the arts and media. Annual subscriptions to *World* are $27.95, and can be ordered by calling 1–800–951-NEWS (6397).

STATE FAMILY POLICY COUNCILS

These state-based family policy councils comprise a national network of independent pro-family research and education organizations dedicated to serving family advocates, legislators and the media.

Alabama

ALABAMA FAMILY ALLIANCE
Gary Palmer
1 Independence Plaza, Suite 322
Birmingham, AL 35209
205–870–9900 (O)
205–870–4407 (FAX)

Arizona

ARIZONA FAMILY RESEARCH INSTITUTE
Trent Franks
First Interstate Tower
3550 N. Central, Suite 1025
Phoenix, AZ 85013
602–277–5181 (O)
602–234–1709 (FAX)

Arkansas

ARKANSAS FAMILY COUNCIL
Jerry Cox
1300 Westpark Drive, Suite 5-B
Little Rock, AR 72204
501–664–4566 (O)
501–664–2317 (FAX)

California

CAPITOL RESOURCE INSTITUTE
Pete Henderson
1211 H Street, Suite A
Sacramento, CA 95814
916–444–8445 (O)
916–447–5191 (FAX)

Colorado

COLORADO FAMILY POLICY INSTITUTE
Tom McMillen
P.O. Box 13619
Denver, CO 80201–3619
303–292–1800 (voice mail)

Connecticut

FAMILY INSTITUTE OF CONNECTICUT
Maraide Prior
56 Woodland Road
New Canaan, CT 06840
203–966–4806 (O & FAX)

Delaware

DELAWARE FAMILY FOUNDATION
Duane Higgins
P.O. Box 3747
Greenville, DE 19807

Florida

FLORIDA FAMILY COUNCIL
Mark Merrill
101 E. Kennedy Blvd., Suite 3120
Tampa, FL 33601
813–222–8300 (O)
813–222–8301 (FAX)

Georgia

GEORGIA FAMILY COUNCIL
2615 Sandy Plains, Suite 100
Marietta, GA 30066
404–977–4673 (O)
404–578–9112 (FAX)

Hawaii

OHANA POLICY CENTER
Rebecca Walker
47–204 Okana Road
P.O. Box 1544
Kaneohe, HI 96744
808–239–4663 (O & FAX)

Idaho

IDAHO FAMILY FORUM
Dennis Mansfield
800 Park Blvd., 5th Floor
P.O. Box 265
Boise, ID 83701
208–386–8101 (O)
208–386–8169 (FAX)

Indiana

INDIANA FAMILY INSTITUTE
Bill Smith
300 N. Meridian, Suite 910
Indianapolis, IN 46204
317–237–2959 (O)
317–237–2957 (FAX)

Kentucky

THE FAMILY FOUNDATION
Kent Ostrander
263 Cochran Road
P.O. Box 22100 (40522)
Lexington, KY 40502
606–255–5400 (O)

Maine

CHRISTIAN CIVIC LEAGUE
Jack Wyman
70 Sewall
P.O. Box 5499 (04332)
Augusta, ME 04330
207–622–7634 (O)
207–622–7635 (FAX)

Massachusetts

PILGRIM FAMILY INSTITUTE
Homer Allen
Wadsworth Village
130 Centre St.
Danvers, MA 01923
508–750–6100 (O)
508–468–6691 (FAX)

Michigan

MICHIGAN FAMILY FORUM
Randall (Randy) Hekman
611 South Walnut
Lansing, MI 48933
517–374–1171 (O)
517–374–6112 (FAX)

Minnesota

THE MINNESOTA FAMILY COUNCIL
Tom Prichard
2875 Snelling Ave. North
St. Paul, MN 55113
612–633–0654 (O)
612–633–4180(FAX)

New Mexico

NEW MEXICO FAMILY FORUM
Pam Wolfe
1250 Lewis
Las Cruces, NM 88001
505–526–8454 (O)
505–526–4930 (FAX)

North Carolina

NORTH CAROLINA FAMILY POLICY COUNCIL
Susan Renfer
3141 John Humphries Wynd, Suite 275
Raleigh, NC 27612
919–787–7723 (O)
919–787–9004 (FAX)

North Dakota

NORTH DAKOTA ALLIANCE
Clinton Birst
P.O. Box 486
Mandan, ND 58554
701–663–2983 (O)
701–663–2990 (FAX)

Ohio

NORTHEASTERN OHIO ROUNDTABLE
David Zanotti
31005 Solon Road
Solon, OH 44139
216–349–3393 (O)
800–522-VOTE (Ohio Only)
216–349–0154 (FAX)

Oklahoma

RESOURCE INSTITUTE OF OKLAHOMA
Terry Allen
28 N.W. 7th Street
Oklahoma City, OK 73102
405–239–6700 (O)

Pennsylvania

PENNSYLVANIA FAMILY INSTITUTE
Mike Geer
600 N. Second St., Suite 400
P.O. Box 220 (17108)
Harrisburg, PA 17101
717–236–2212 (O)
717–231–4854 (FAX)

South Dakota

SOUTH DAKOTA FAMILY VALUES INSTITUTE
Ed Glassgow
P.O. Box 1580
Rapid City, SD 57709–1580
605–343–6917 (O)
605–342–2053 (FAX)

Tennessee

FAMILY ACTION COALITION OF TENNESSEE
David R. Shepherd
8005 Church Street East
Brentwood, TN 37027
615–371–0707(O)
615–661–4862 (FAX)

Texas

FREE MARKET FOUNDATION
Richard Ford
P.O. Box 741777
Dallas, TX 75374
214–348–2801 (O)
214–348–6725 (FAX)

Virginia

FAMILY FOUNDATION
Walt Barbee, Chairman
8001 Forbes Place, Suite 102
Springfield, VA 22151
703–321–8338 (O)
703–321–8408 (FAX)

Washington

FAMILY VALUES ALLIANCE
Doug Burman
9618 Gravelly Lake Dr., S.W.
P.O. Box 99055
Tacoma, WA 98499
(206) 584–3788 (O)
(206) 582–6541 (FAX)